THE
ITALIAN LAKES

GABRIEL FAURE

THE
ITALIAN LAKES

Translated by GEORGE MILLARD

Cover design by DESPIERRE

169 heliogravure illustrations

NICHOLAS KAYE
LONDON

FIRST PUBLISHED IN ENGLISH
BY NICHOLAS KAYE LTD.,
BISHOPSGATE, LONDON E. C. 2,
1958

FIRST PUBLISHED IN FRENCH BY
B. ARTHAUD PARIS AND GRENOBLE
UNDER THE TITLE
AUX LACS ITALIENS

PRINTED IN FRANCE

CONTENTS

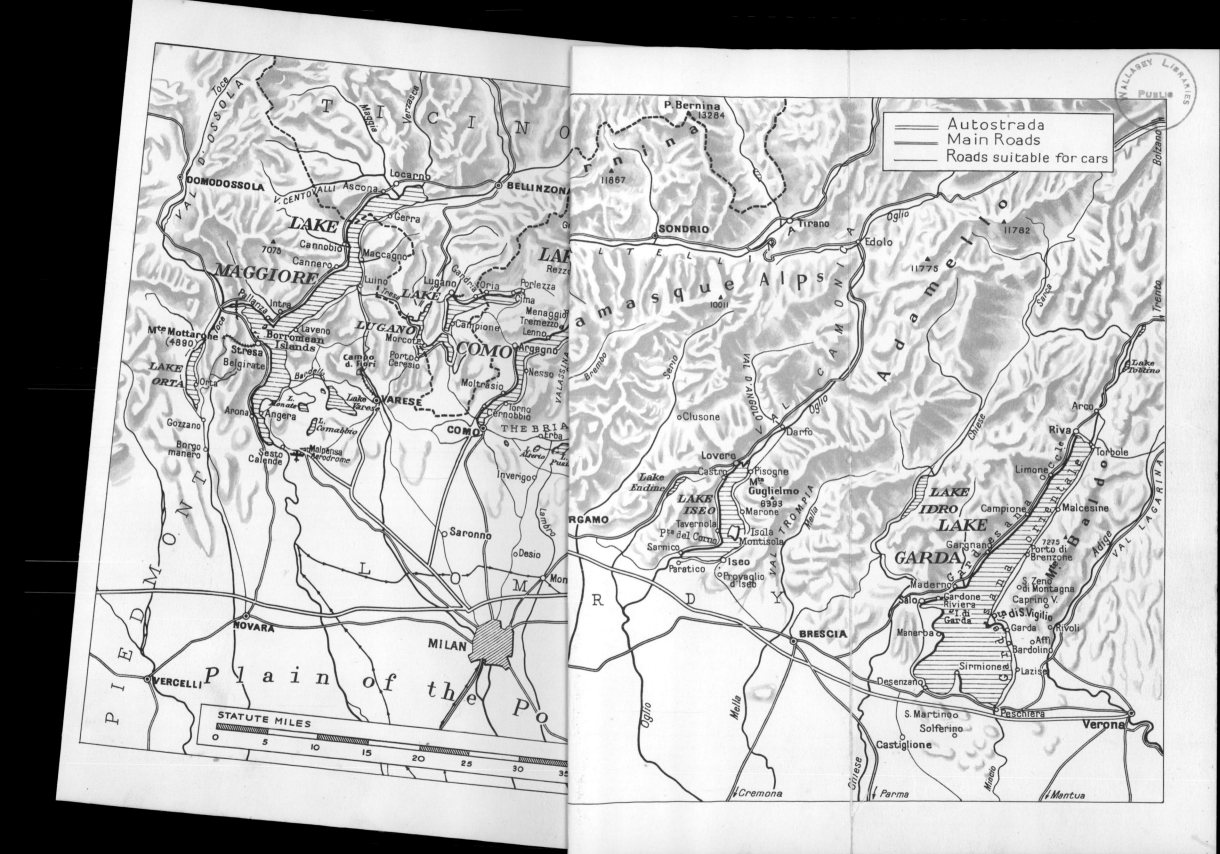

Autostrada
Main Roads
Roads suitable for cars

P. Bernina
13284

T I C I N O

VAL D'OSSOLA

Toce

Maggia

Verzasca

DOMODOSSOLA

V. CENTOVALLI   Ascona   Locarno

BELLINZONA

LAKE

Gerra

7075   Cannobio

Cannero   Maccagno

MAGGIORE

Luino   Gandria   Oria   Porlezza

Pallanza   Intra   Tresa   LAKE   Lugano   Cima

Mte Mottarone   Laveno   LUGANO   Campione   Menaggio
(4890)   Morcote   Tremezzo
Stresa   Borromean   Porto   Lenno
Belgirate   Islands   Campo   Ceresio   Argegno
d. Fiori   COMO
Bardello   Nesso
LAKE   Lake
ORTA   Varese   VARESE   Moltrasio
Orta   L.   THE BRIA
Monate   Torno   Erba
Gozzano   Arona   Angera   COMO   Cernobbio
L.   L.O.
Borgo   Comabbio   Alserio
manero   Sesto   Malpensa   Inverigo   L.
Calende   Aerodrome   Pusi

PIEDMONT

L

Saronno

Desio

M

Mon

SONDRIO   Tirano
Edolo
11867   11782
11775
amasque Alps   Adamello
10011
VAL CAMONICA
Brembo   Senio   VAL D'ANGOLO   Oglio   Chiese
Clusone   Darfo
VAL TROMPIA   Arco
Lovere   Lake
Castro   Pisogne   Tobl
Lake   Mta   Riva
Endine   Gugliemo   Limone   Torbole
LAKE   6393   Campione   Malcesine
ISEO   Marone   LAKE
Tavernola   Isola   IDRO   7275
RGAMO   Pta del Corno   Montisola   LAKE   Porto di
Sarnico   Gargnano   Brenzone
Iseo   GARDA   S. Zeno
Paratico   Provaglio   Maderno   di Montagna
d'Iseo   Salo   Caprino V.
R   Gardone   te di S.Vigilio
Riviera   Garda   Rivoli
D   I. di   Affi
Y   BRESCIA   Garda   Bardolino
Manerba   Sirmione   Lazise
Desenzano
NOVARA   Verona
Bolzano
VERCELLI   P l a i n   o f   t h e   P o   MILAN   S. Martino   Peschiera   VERONA
Solferino
Castiglione   Mincio

STATUTE MILES
0   5   10   15   20   25   30   35

Oglio   Mella   Chiese   Mincio
Cremona   Parma   Mantua

Adige   VAL LAGARINA
Lake
Toblino
Mte Baldo

" What can one say about Lake Maggiore, about the Borromean Islands, about Lake Como, unless it be that one pities those who are not madly in love with them ? "

STENDHAL.

BESIDE THE ROAD FROM RIVA DI GARDA TO TRENTO.   THE TINY LAKE OF TOBLINO.

ON THE SHORES OF LAKE COMO.

CHAPTER ONE

THE LAKES REVISITED

It is often far pleasanter, " I once wrote somewhere, " to return
and see a place again than to discover it. " To find oneself back
in a well-loved town or to contemplate afresh a beautiful landscape
gives the same pleasure as re-reading a favourite book in which one
constantly meets previously unnoticed delights, new reasons for loving

9

and admiring it. Isn't this especially true of the Italian Lakes?
Having visited and described them so frequently, I always revisit
them with undiminished pleasure. The Italian Lakes : I am quite
sure there are no words more evocative. The syllables of these
melodious names have, for me, a magical quality. During the too-
bleak, tardy spring days in Paris how can one fail to dream

LAKE COMO. SPURANO.

TWILIGHT AT RIVA DI GARDA.

of the shores of Stresa and Bellagio, already flower-strewn, of those avenues of the Villa Carlotta flanked, from April onwards, with the dense varnished buds of azaleas and rhododendrons ? But perhaps the spell is most potent at summer's end. When I half-close my eyes, the better to recall and enjoy my impressions, mental images glide before me. I see beautiful terraced gardens, oleander bushes smothered in blossom, white boats on the blue water, bright villas surrounded by cypresses, by olive and chestnut groves... In a matter of hours I have packed my lug-

MALCESINE AND LAKE GARDA.

gage and booked my seat. The same evening, in the outward-bound train, I dream of the morrow's wonderful awakening when, emerging from the Simplon, I shall see the Borromean Islands.

•

For the new edition of this book I wanted to see the Lakes again, not as a hurrying tourist who admired them hastily, in passing, fountain-

THE CAMPANILE OF SANTA MARIA MADDALENA AT OSPEDALETTO,
OPPOSITE THE ISOLA COMACINA ON LAKE COMO.

THE GARDESANA OCCIDENTALE.

pen in hand, but as a conscientious writer eager to compare his memories
and earlier impressions with present-day feelings.   It seemed that Nature

BETWEEN LIMONE AND GARGNANO. ESPALIER CULTIVATION.

THE SHORES OF LAKE GARDA AT LIMONE.

was a willing accomplice. If it was not actually raining while we crossed the Valais — as it so often is — it was so dreary and grey all along the upper Rhône valley that I fully appreciated the joy of the light and the sight of the little market town of Iselle glittering in the sunshine on the far side of the tunnel.

Descending the Italian hillsides is always pleasurable and I love the welcome of these villages of the Cenis, Simplon, St Gotthard or Brenner Passes. They combine Alpine grandeur with southern mildness. Whether one enters Italy by train or by motor car, nothing is more enjoyable than this first contact with *Terra Latina,* above all when one has traversed a Switzerland already shrouded in thick September fog. Who does not recall Goethe's enthusiasm when he reached the Brenner and saluted the very dust on the Italian roads ? On the road from the Simplon the aged Alexandre Dumas would begin to digress as soon as he felt the first puffs of breeze from Lombardy, and observed the white, flat-roofed houses, like swans warming themselves in the sun. The closer he approached to the shores of Lake Maggiore the more his excitement used to bubble over. " At each step one meets pretty wine-harvesters, with pale complexions, velvety eyes, quick soft voices, " he cried, " the sky is pure, the air mild and one recognizes the land beloved of the gods, the happy land that neither barbarous invasions nor civil discords could deprive of its heaven sent blessings. "

It seems as though the most skilful of stage managers had set the scene, placing the Italian Lakes in exactly the right spot to create the maximum effect. Neither the Lakes of Savoy nor the Swiss Lakes so readily endear themselves : they are too cold, too austere and often too awe-inspiring. They lack that combination of nobility with special charm, that exactness of proportions and above all that languor that one finds scarcely anywhere but on these Alpine slopes facing Italy. Part of their charm consists in this mixture — or rather this juxtaposition — of Alpine and southern landscapes. It is still Switzerland when the high peaks overhanging these shores are all white and when the snowflakes come to prevent the spring from arriving too soon. But it is already Italy with the melodious tones of its language, with its coloured campaniles proclaiming the gaiety of a religion that knows no sadness — with its bright roads cluttered with carts, whose drivers, stretched full length on the awnings covering their wares, lie sleeping in the warm torpor of the midday sunshine.

ARCO. A PAIR OF OXEN NEAR LAKE GARDA.

There is nothing more pleasant than to drive along the magnificent roads which, following the curving shorelines, almost completely encircle the Italian Lakes. The gently rippling water sparkles in the brilliant sunlight like a spangled silken fabric, and the gardens stretch lazily down to its very edge. Vines flow from tree to tree. The lower slopes are clothed with the dull grey of olive trees, relieved by the green of oaks and chestnuts higher up. Still higher, bare mountains are sharply etched against a sky so intensely blue that it has a metallic gleam re-

IN THE GARDENS OF THE VILLA D'ESTE AT CERNOBBIO, LAKE COMO.

miniscent of those blues the primitives used to paint behind the heads of their Madonnas.

A GARDEN AT LIMONE.

But the height of luxury is to sail on the lakes in one of those gracefully hooped boats which are to be found in all the little lakeside harbours. Rocked by the monotonous movement of the waves, one watches, as in a dream, the land and the bright houses, sparkling in the sunlight, receding in a golden haze. A few villages on the hillsides cling round their campaniles like swallows' nests on the edge of a roof. The water shimmers so brightly that one seems to be gliding on plate glass. There is a warm breeze, languid with the fragrance of departing summer. An occasional puff of wind, especially when the boat passes near a garden where *olea fragrans* is in flower, bears a perfume so heavy that one seems to be sailing through a cloud of incense.

Water always softens the harshness of a landscape and gives it an indefinable, carefree charm. But the special enchantment of these lakes, usually quite narrow and elongated between hills, derives from the fact that these limit the horizon, so that the eye is arrested by precise objects. All along the Mediterranean coasts, on the Riviera, at Naples, Palermo or Corfu, equally beautiful gardens bask in the languid atmosphere, beside equally blue water. One can enjoy there the delights of living among panoramas just as wonderful. The sea even increases their majesty. But precisely because of this majesty, of its immensity, above all of its changeableness, the effect is less direct — in a sense less physical. There is no limit to the view nor to one's dreams. The sea offers too many unknown possibilities. It is not, as the lake is, on the same scale as our view or as our desires. The sea is like a woman who dances afar off before an ever-changing backcloth, indifferent to those who are watching. The Italian lakes are like beautiful girls who come to meet us, like those nymphs whose supple and elegant bearing Politian praised : *il dolce andar soave*. I can never look at Botticelli's *Primavera* without imagining that it was painted in the grove of a villa at Bellagio, where the immediate presence of the water contributes a languor sometimes lacking in Tuscan landscapes.

●

To enjoy the Italian lakes to the full one must, as I have pointed out, visit them in either spring or autumn. In March, when one has crossed the Alps still buffeted by snowstorms, not only does the sun gladden one's whole being : there is the added joy of springtime beauty, of which one can never weary. Never are the mountains that bound the horizon outlined more sharply ; and one muses on that *lumine acuto* of which Dante speaks when he extols the skies of his native land.

TERRACES OF THE ISOLA BELLA, LAKE MAGGIORE.

So pure is the atmosphere, as yet unsullied by summer dust-storms, that one can observe the minutest variations in the relief of the terrain. The hills, that close the shores so harmoniously without confining them, take on delicate hues : their shapely curves, like young breasts, and their supple undulations are revealed more clearly than in the autumn. They are not hidden by the unvarying colour of the leafless tree branches. The snow, which still covers all the summits, picks out the crests and peaks against the blue sky. After April's first smiling day, what a feast

ENTRANCE TO THE GARDENS OF THE VILLA CARLOTTA, LAKE COMO.

PAPYRUS IN THE GARDENS OF THE VILLA CARLOTTA.

for the eyes when the flowering fruit trees throw their dazzling and splendid garlands around the shores ! The bursting of blossom from every tree bole calls to mind the poetry of springtime in Japan. The petals of falling cherry blossom bestrew the ground like snowdrifts. Nearby the pink peach, white pear and yellow-tinged plum trees seem to have brought out their ball dresses. Here and there square fields of rape sparkle in the sun like shining copper coins. In the pale green hedges and fields, beside streams and on the banks of ditches, there are great masses of primroses, of buttercups, of black-fringed red anemones, of pink ranunculus, of narcissi and of all those humble meadow flowers whose names I have never known.

Still more intense is the delight of the gardens where the orange trees bear flowers and fruits simultaneously, where the Australian magnolias display their delicately poised corollas and the giant camellias unfold their glossy petals. The mimosas that adorn the last days of winter have withered ; but the azaleas are about to flower. In the warmest corners, on the terraces of the Villa Carlotta or of the Isola Madre, a few premature rhododendrons are already raising their brilliant nosegays. This splendid fairyland, this exquisite magic, surpasses anything the Mediterranean shores can offer, for — save in very rare spots — the high mountains are too far from the sea. Here all things conspire to delight the eye ! Nowhere else does the joy of rebirth proclaim itself so clamorously. On the Riviera, where there is practically no winter, spring is but little appreciated. Here it is, for several weeks, entirely bewitching. The peach trees wave their pink sashes beneath the frost-spangled forests just as in the Christmas fables ; and now and then snowflakes settle on the red flowers of the first camellias...

●

And yet, save that the eye is completely enchanted in springtime, the Italian lakes are at their most richly poetic, most incomparably alluring, only in autumn when the languor and perfumes of the departing summer drift around them like everlasting incense.

One dreams of the gardens of Armida where Tasso's hero felt his hatred being charmed into love by the fragrance of the flowers. These shores are at times so intoxicatingly beautiful as to make true lovers almost regret a needless conspiracy and delights that are not derived solely from their own passion.

But alas ! Each year the character of these famous beauty-spots

27

SIRMIONE.   THE MOATS, THE DRAWBRIDGE AND THE CASTLE OF THE SCALIGER FAMILY.

RIVA DI GARDA. THE TORRE APPONALE.

LAKE ORTA AND THE ISOLA SAN GIULIO.

is changing and almost invariably for the worse. Each time I return I find fresh things that sadden me. How the lakes have changed between the occasion of my first journey of discovery and the present day ! Masses of hotels, of villas, of houses of all kinds have sprung up beside the roads so that often, in the pleasantest and sunniest corners, they stretch like town streets right along the shore. Already there are places where the roads are entirely built up and so crowded with cars and vans that one can no longer travel in comfort on foot : for instance between Como and Cernobbio and between Baveno and Stresa. But then who has time to saunter these days ? It must be admitted that one can cover all the roads of the region in a few days by car. One sees less well, and in less detail ; but one does see far more. And above all one is not restricted to those scenes visible from the shores. One can scale the neighbouring heights whence wider views, often vast stretches of countryside, can be seen.

The boats which, formerly, were almost the only means of visiting the lakes are nowadays hardly used except to cross from one shore to the other. Buses follow the lakeside roads and link up the villages. One still takes the boat in order to go from Bellagio to Menaggio or from Luino to Stresa ; but for preference one travels by car from Como to Menaggio or from Arona to Baveno.

The loveliest beauty-spots among the lakes, cluttered with buildings, are gradually losing the charm they once had. Sadly, a slow but sure death from its very glory is the price paid for the beauty of these too magnificent shores : like that laurel on the Borromean Islands on which, according to legend, Napoleon had carved the word " Victory " on the eve of Marengo and which could not survive the mutilations inflicted by over-zealous admirers.

Happily there are still corners away from the main roads whose very position protects — and will continue to protect — them from invasion and hurly-burly. Under the cypresses of Bellagio or the arbours of the Isola dei Pescatori — and, even better, on still little-known shores such as those of Orta or Iseo — day-dreamers, if any remain, can still enjoy the pleasures of solitude with memories of the time when only the sound of the paddle-steamers disturbed the silence of these tranquil shores. After all, it is not so long ago : they may possibly remember it.

●

The lakes of Northern Italy, sometimes described as the " Lombardy Lakes ", do not, however, belong entirely to Lombardy or even, at

FISHERMAN AT LENNO. LAKE COMO.

times, to Italy. Lake Orta and the western half of Lake Maggiore are part of Piedmont. The eastern half of Lake Garda belongs, at least administratively, to Venetia. The northern tip of Lake Maggiore and a large part of Lake Lugano are in Switzerland. But because they form an entity as the result of a common geological history it is legitimate to group them in one survey.

Before the Ice Age, the plain of the River Po was a bay on the Adriatic flanked by fiords where the present-day lakes are. The deepest parts of these lakes are often below sea-level and the fact that various salt-water fish are found in their waters can only be explained by this hypothesis. When huge glaciers came down from the Alps they filled the cavities of the lakes and rolled on right into the Lombardy Plain, where

LAKE MAGGIORE. THE ISOLA DEI PESCATORI. FISHING BOATS.

AT PELLA, ON THE SHORES OF LAKE ORTA.

their moraines can still be clearly seen. During the thousands of years the Ice Age lasted the plain gradually pushed upwards and the sea retreated correspondingly. When the glaciers receded, the fiords — no longer joined to the sea — progressively filled with fresh water. Their overflow made its way into the Adriatic either by rivers flowing straight into the Po or else by way of a neighbouring lake at a lower level. For example Lakes Orta and Varese both flow into Lake Maggiore.

RIVA DI GARDA. A LEMON-SELLER.

LAKE ORTA AT SUNSET.

ORTA AND THE LAKE.

CHAPTER TWO

THE LAKES OF ORTA AND VARESE

L ake Orta is the first to be seen and admired by the traveller who comes through the Simplon, by road or railway, and branches westwards before reaching Lake Maggiore. Less wild than Lake Lugano, less voluptuous than Lake Como, less spectacular than Lake Maggiore or Lake Garda, it has a greater sense of harmony than any of the others.

37

Everything is just as it should be, with no discordant note. The curves and folds of the wooded hills that surround it harmonize perfectly with the lake's meandering shores. Its Isola San Giulio epitomizes in itself the diverse beauties of the Borromean Islands. The Punta d'Orta is almost as charming as the promontory of Bellagio. And the lake has retained something which its more famous rivals — slowly but surely invaded and despoiled by what is called civilization — no longer possess : the tranquillity of nature. One can listen for hours to the lapping of the water undisturbed by the vibrations of motor traffic ; two or three little boats are sufficient to serve the harbours. Very seldom do motor cars stray as far as its shores, far away from the main road. I was one of the first to extol it : I even introduced some Italians to it.

On the first occasion that I spoke of Lake Orta, forty years ago, I expressed the fear that this almost unknown Arcadia might soon succumb to invasion by tourists. I had heard some of the lakeside residents complain that their lake was always called *Cenerentola* (Cinderella) because it remained forgotten beside its larger brothers. How delighted I was to rediscover Orta scarcely modernized and almost as deserted as before ! It is true that some Italians return faithfully every year, but these are chiefly quiet, sensible people who have chosen this delightful setting for carefree rest. Hurrying tourists will never turn aside from their route to linger and enjoy its peace and quiet.

Lake Orta, situated at a height of about 1,000 feet, has one peculiarity : its overflow runs from the south northwards instead of flowing, as do all the other water-courses, towards the plain of the Po. The reason is that this one empties into Lake Maggiore, the level of which is about 330 feet lower than that of Orta.

To visit Lake Orta, if one approaches from France by the Simplon line, one must leave the express at Domodossola and follow the old line towards Novara which one took long ago when travelling by coach from the Simplon. The line that leads direct to Lake Maggiore, towards Baveno and Stresa, was not constructed until after the tunnel was opened. After crossing the River Toce and skirting the western flank of Monte Mottarone, the Orta line reaches the lake at Omegna, a busy commercial and industrial centre. The thirteenth-century parish church of Sant'-Ambrogio has an elegant campanile which looks well when the little town is seen from the lake.

The villages which occur at intervals all along the shores have little of interest for the curious visitor. But he may well be content with

Orta, delightfully situated at the foot of a sort of hilly peninsula with only the narrowest strip along the water's edge on which the houses perch. The little town, which gave the lake its name, has a population of scarcely more than 1100 ; it is really nothing more than a long street parallel to the shore, with a shady piazzetta adorned by a tiny late sixteenth-century Municipium where the Council-General of the Lake used formerly to meet. The first floor is reached by an

ALZO. THE STATIONS OF THE CROSS AND CHURCH OF SAN FILIBERTO
IN THE GROUNDS OF THE OLD CEMETERY.

THE ISOLA SAN GIULIO.

outside staircase which gives a picturesque air to the little building.

The slopes of the hill overlooking Orta are strewn with villas surrounded by those luxuriant shrubs that one finds in every sheltered corner of the Italian Lakes. Rhododendrons, azaleas, oleanders display their superb blossoms. Fig trees exhale their slightly bitter odour beside the roads leading down to the lake. Through their broad leaves one glimpses the sparkling water and the little island of San Giulio quivering and smiling in the brilliant sunlight. How can I resist the desire to see again, at once, this miracle which formerly cast such a powerful spell over me ?

Within minutes a boat is on its way there, and as it moves closer, so the spell works. Terraces and gardens seem to hang above the lake in which, at a great depth, the campanile and the high walls of the seminary are reflected. The leafy groves that frame the houses give the islet an air of gaiety. Throughout the nineteenth century this was the headquarters of the township of Orta. As it comprised the town hall, the church and the cemetery, the baptismal, marriage and burial processions, for all those who did not live on the island, took place by boat, as at Venice. Not until 1918 was the position reversed and the little palazzo on the piazza became the Municipium for the entire township. But the parish of San Giulio was not suppressed and at certain times religious services still occasion the coming and going of boats and canoes across the lake.

Space on the island is so limited that buildings are piled one above the other and not a scrap of land is wasted. A single narrow road, or rather pathway, between the houses or the tiny gardens encircles the island. The general effect is most strange and one may hope that it will not be spoiled for a very long time to come.

The basilica of San Giulio is of great interest. Its foundation dates back to the fourth century, when St Julius came to rid the island of a dragon and some serpents which had invaded it. Rebuilt in the ninth and tenth centuries, it still possesses some columns, capitals and low-relief carvings of that period. But the most notable work of art is a Romanesque pulpit of solid black marble carved with the emblems of the four evangelists and two curious panels on which Christianity and paganism are symbolized respectively by a griffin and a crocodile triumphing over one another in turn. If this interpretation, given me by the caretaker on my first visit, be correct, the sculptor was certainly a man who could deal tactfully with the future...

Numerous frescoes adorn the pillars, vaults and walls of the chapels,

THE ISOLA SAN GIULIO. THE TWELFTH-CENTURY CHURCH PULPIT.

the best being the work of Gaudenzio Ferrari, the fine painter born on the far side of the mountain which overhangs the western shore of the lake, at Valduggia. One can reach this spot in a few hours by crossing the saddle of the Colma through a forest of those old chestnut trees which adorn the Alps of Piedmont. Gaudenzio Ferrari would be a

THE FLIGHT INTO EGYPT. A DETAIL OF THE FRESCO BY GAUDENZIO FERRARI
IN THE CHURCH ON THE ISOLA SAN GIULIO.

celebrated artist in any other country : but Renaissance Italy is so rich in painters that she has rather neglected him. His fame has scarcely spread beyond the region in which — admittedly — the majority of his paintings still remain. We shall meet him again, and have a chance to study his work still further beside Lake Maggiore, particularly at Cannobio, and in Como Cathedral. On a previous visit I had made a point of going to pay my respects to him in his birthplace, and at Varallo, a pleasant village on the Sesia, which possesses many of his works.

Gaudenzio Ferrari is, like his fellow-countryman Luini, a master of fresco painting. He has, perhaps, less grace than his famous rival but more action, more power in his paintings and, considering his period, one finds details of a quite daring naturalism, some of which detract from the emotional effect. One recognizes in him an artist torn between the somewhat primitive inclinations derived from his mountainous background and the idealism introduced from Florence to Milan by Leonardo da Vinci ; but — and this, to my mind, entitles him to distinction — Ferrari, having scarcely ever left the banks of the Sesia and the shores of Lake Maggiore and Lake Orta, was more successful than other artists in resisting Leonardo's influence and retaining his native integrity.

His frescoes fill an entire chapel in the church of San Giulio. They comprise : on the rear wall, the *Virgin Surrounded by Saints* and the *Martyrdom of St Stephen;* on the ceiling, the four *Evangelists;* on the vault, four *Prophets;* on the pillars, on one side : *St Michael and St Appolonia;* on the other, *St Julius and one of his Companions.* All the figures are of excellent workmanship. Unfortunately these frescoes concealed earlier works, still being discovered; in some places one can even detect the remnants of a still more ancient painting on which the other two have been superimposed. Perhaps an attempt will be made, using modern techniques, to expose these earlier decorations, removing elsewhere Gaudenzio Ferrari's works, which are already grievously damaged by the weather and by the stupidity of visitors who have insisted on carving their names on them. Let us console — no, rather sadden — ourselves by noticing that this is not just a present-day habit : the caretaker showed me, and with a certain pride, signatures and dates of 1536 and 1541 — that is, almost contemporaneous with the paintings...

In the crypt beneath the transept is the sarcophagus containing the relics of St Julius. In the sacristy are more pictures and a bone of the famous dragon which the saint exterminated. But to be truthful I am in a hurry to see the lake again. The sun is shining brilliantly. In the still, unruffled water the villages and hills are perfectly reflected. The water is smoothly green like molten emeralds, reminding one of Dante's beautiful imagery when he compares it to *fresco smeraldo a l'ora che si fiacco.*

44

THE MUNICIPIO, ORTA (LATE SIXTEENTH CENTURY).

And then, before the close of day, I want to climb the wooded slope,
extending in a promontory towards the lake, whose summit and flanks
are occupied by a *Sacro Monte*, of which there are several in the region.

Let us, in passing, admire the wrought-iron cemetery gates. Previously, on the island and in the streets of Orta I had observed many

45

balconies produced in the forges of the seventeenth and eighteenth centuries. There are, notably, some magnificent grilles in the church of San Giulio ; but none that compares with the great gateway to the cemetery. What superbly elegant yet supple lines ! This is undoubtedly a very fine specimen of decorative art.

The twenty shrines of the Sacro Monte, built between 1591 and 1770, enclose groups in painted terracotta depicting the chief events in the life of St Francis, and frescoes representing episodes in the Old and New Testaments. There is nothing especially noteworthy about any of them and one need not study them in detail. But the site on which the twenty shrines stand is delightful. It is a sort of huge park that covers the entire hill. At each turn in the paths one gets glimpses of the varied aspects of the lake. One instinctively thinks of the pathways of the Villa Serbelloni which look out in turn upon the three arms of

THE SACRO MONTE, ORTA.

A CHAPEL ON THE SACRO MONTE, ORTA.

Lake Como. But here the impression is more austere for there is an
abundance of religious pictures and but few flowers. Even the trees
take on an air of solemnity. Huge pines, with trunks straight and smooth
like columns, elms, beeches, thrust upward into the light of the dying
day ; the little white chapels seem to be leaning against the stout pillars

of their cathedral. Already the villages clustered at the foot of the slopes are blurred in a haze of blue dust. The lake nestles in the dark bowl of the mountains which enfold it with their harmonious lines. On the far side, above Pella, slumbering in its bed of chestnut and walnut trees, rises the extreme tip of Monte Rosa.

●

Before we undertake our visit to Lake Maggiore, let us go to see a group of four small lakes to the south of Lake Lugano, of which Lake Varese is the chief. The other three are hardly more than satellites. But if a car is available one should turn aside from the main road for a quick but not unpleasing visit.

One comes first upon Lake Comabbio, also sometimes named after Verano, the little village that stands on its northern shore. As it is not more than about 24 feet deep it is often used for fish-breeding.

Lake Monate is certainly more picturesque : in 1864 the remains of lakeside buildings on piles were discovered there.

Further to the north the tiny Lake Biandronno is separated from that of Varese only by a narrow tongue of land which carries the road that encircles the latter lake, an easy drive of about 17 miles which shows how small is the area of this lake. Its importance results from its closeness to Varese : it benefits from the fame enjoyed by this pretty town with its Sacro Monte and celebrated Campo dei Fiori. Both of these hills must be climbed for the superb views obtainable from their summits over the whole group of lakes.

There are few towns in Italy more pleasing than Varese, a gay, prosperous, lively town (it has 60,000 inhabitants), teeming with people on the occasions of its important markets and horse fairs. Its neighbourhood is one of the most delightful corners of Lombardy ; and to the people of Milan it is one of their chosen holiday haunts. Many of them have built themselves luxurious villas there surrounded by well-wooded parklands. As it is seldom visited by foreign tourists except on feast-days and fair-days, one can take one's ease there in complete comfort and enjoy the quiet dignity of its public gardens, which are among the finest in Northern Italy.

But before going to saunter there let us swiftly inspect the town and especially its basilica of San Vittore, rebuilt at the end of the sixteenth century by Pellegrino Tibaldi. This same great architect designed the tall isolated campanile, with its massive granite plinth, whence one

THE CAMPANILE OF THE CHURCH OF SAN VITTORE, VARESE.

can look out upon Varese, the lake and the surrounding countryside. The baptistery of San Giovanni just behind this will interest archaeologists.

The public garden is the park of the former Corte which Francesco III d'Este, Duke of Modena, had built in the mid-eighteenth century. The

A VILLA AT VARESE.

palace now houses the Prefecture, the Municipium and the Library.

The park, planted in the old Italian manner, has great nobility and austere dignity. Its lawns are framed in centuries-old hornbeam hedges. I recall having seen it one year in the spring when it was filled with the luxuriant blossom of camellias, chestnuts, glossy-leaved Australian

THE PUBLIC GARDENS, VARESE.

THE SACRO MONTE, VARESE.

magnolias and lilacs. In the autumn the odours that hover around the groves are both heavier and more subtle. The riotous colour of the dahlia-beds outshines the reddish ochre walls of the old palace. In the background a mound shaded by pines and cedars gives still greater character and grandeur to the garden : the view from the highest terrace stretches away to the western Alps dominated by Monte Rosa. On the way back one sees above the roofs of the town the Tre Croci, the Madonna del Monte and the Campo dei Fiori, all of them ascents which should be made. This is easy nowadays because all these summits can be reached by motor car. I recall climbing the Madonna del Monte on my first trip in an oxcart up a rough Path of the Cross with endless hairpin bends. It was slow going. But how much more enjoyable to ascend gradually and to discover at each fresh turn an ever wider view !

Extensive views over the whole region may be seen from the Tre Croci, 3600 feet high, and there are still better views from the Campo dei Fiori, over 3950 feet. But from the Sacro Monte, only 2800 feet up, the views are almost as beautiful. And the tourist pressed for time or without a car might well limit himself to this last climb, visiting some of the fifteen shrines of the famous pilgrimage. These resemble those of the Sacro Monte at Orta except that they are larger, with a portico and a flight of steps in front. The groups of terracotta statues and the seventeenth-century paintings depicting the mysteries of the Rosary, which frame them, are works of no great merit and need not be examined closely.

I understand why the fine view from the summit has excited many travellers. One sees a great part of Lombardy almost to Milan, which one imagines on the horizon, including six lakes ; to the left Lake Como ; in front, that of Varese ; to the right the little lakes of Biandronno, Monate and Comabbio ; lastly, far beyond, two bits of Maggiore. Doubtless Stendhal included these when he counted up to seven lakes and exclaimed : " A magnificent group... one might traverse France and Germany and not find a comparable sight ! " Perhaps our novelist sometimes found the countryside less splendid... It was in fact here, at the Madonna del Monte, that he suffered one of his cruellest sentimental disappointments. He had come in holiday mood to see once more Angelina Pietragrua whom he had known in his youth when he first visited Milan ; and whom he had just found again, looking even lovelier than he had imagined during the years of separation. But the Madonna del Monte no longer favoured him and he was unable to rejoin his pretty Milanese,

A GARDEN AT VARESE.

who contrived to escape him by pleading her husband's jealousy... So here, on this very terrace, perhaps seated on this same parapet, Stendhal awaited in vain the woman whom he dubbed a " hussy " and berated even more forcibly. Doubtless there are some tourists who climb Sacro Monte for whom this memory will have a special significance.

The lake itself, which is invisible from Varese, is a sheet of water with rather flat unattractive surroundings. It owes something of its reputation, at any rate among artists and men of letters, firstly to Stendhal as I have already explained, but also to a somewhat ambiguous phrase of Taine's which made Maurice Barrès, in particular, believe that the philosopher would have liked to have a country villa by Lake Varese. In fact, however, Taine did not come very close to its shores but contented himself with the view of it from the top of the road leading to Laveno on Lake Maggiore. And it so happens that from the road, especially when one is travelling from Milan, one suddenly comes upon the most harmonious view : the lake in the foreground ; Varese and its suburbs on the wooded hillsides, the Madonna del Monte, the Tre Croci, the Campo dei Fiori, and, to the left, beyond Lake Maggiore, Monte Mottarone and the glaciers of Monte Rosa, which in all this region of the lakes contribute to the landscape — sometimes too pretty and too languorous — the awful sternness of the high Alps.

THE WROUGHT-IRON GATE OF THE CEMETERY AT ORTA.

THE ISOLA BELLA SEEN FROM STRESA.

THE FONTANA DEI PUTTI IN THE GARDENS OF THE VILLA TARANTO, PALLANZA.

CHAPTER THREE

LAKE MAGGIORE

The area of the former *Lacus Verbanus* is over 125 square miles, or almost twice that of the Lake of Lucerne. Its shape is that of a narrow, elongated sack ; and it is 37 ½ miles long, by 2 to 3 miles wide, swelling to a sort of gigantic pouch at the point where the Borromean

Islands occur. Many rivers flow into this great trough, which is well over 1000 feet deep in many places. First there are all the waters of the whole mountainous region which stretches from the St Gotthard

THE MADONNA DEL SASSO, LOCARNO.

THE LAKE SHORE AT LOCARNO BY NIGHT.

to Monte Rosa brought by the rivers Ticino, Verzasca and Maggia, to name only the most important streams. Next there are those which bring the overflow from the neighbouring lakes : the Bardello issuing from Lake Varese, the Tresa from Lake Lugano and the Toce which pours in both the waters from the Val d'Ossola and those from Lake Orta. All these tributaries, sometimes swollen simultaneously by storms, raise the level of the lake by many feet, causing disastrous floods round its shores.

The river which carries away the waters of Lake Maggiore is still called the Ticino. It flows out near Sesto Calende, a broad navigable waterway bright blue in colour, like the Rhône flowing out of the Lake

RIVAPIANA. NEAR LOCARNO.

GERRA.

AT CANNOBIO.

of Geneva. After traversing part of the Plain of Lombardy —
where it supplies an ingenious system of irrigation canals — it joins

the Po near Pavia, where a famous covered bridge links its two banks.

The shores of Lake Maggiore offer an infinite variety of picturesque scenery — now wild, now luxuriant, now bounded by sheer rugged mountains, now falling away almost level with the plain. The lake itself is continually changing. I have seen it slumbering, green and transparent in calm grandeur ; an hour later it was dark and forbidding, lashed by great waves driven before the wind.

The shores of the northern end, which incidentally belongs to the Swiss Republic, look like a Swiss lake with just an odd Italian corner. Although situated uneasily at the foot of high mountains, Locarno is very southern in aspect. Formerly the town stretched alongside the lake but the latter has been gradually receding and the silt deposited year by year by the unruly river Maggia constantly increases the gap. Possibly the upper part of the lake may one day be severed from the rest : indeed perhaps within a few centuries the soil brought down by the rivers Ticino, Maggia and Verzasca will fill it completely. The old castle of Locarno to the south-west of the town — one of Northern Italy's strongest fortresses when the township belonged to the Duchy of Milan — had a harbour which linked it to the lake. This is now nothing but a muddy pond full of aquatic plants. The castle is surrounded by stretches of alluvial soil called *salicetti* — gravel beds in which willows flourish.

Locarno, with its suburbs of Muralto and Minusio, is a fine town of some seven to eight thousand inhabitants and belongs to the Swiss canton of Ticino. It used at one time to share, turn and turn about, with Lugano and Bellinzona, the honour of being capital : Bellinzona has remained the canton's chief town. Cowering beneath steep 6500-feet-high mountains it stretches itself languidly in the sunshine. The narrow strip of shore is like an espalier against a wall : cold winds blow above it leaving it quite unscathed. Its mild healthy climate, with an average temperature slightly above that of Lugano, makes it a very popular winter resort, where superb camellias and magnolias remain in flower throughout the winter. Every year in April the camellia festival is held. Some of the trees in the Franzoni Garden are as fine as any in the region. Tourists seldom leave the town without going to see the Pretorio Palace where the famous Locarno Conference took place in 1925.

Behind the town is a river bed, usually dry, between high banks — that of the Ramogna — which a second ravine enters not far away. On the cliff separating the two gorges stands the fifteenth-century

63

THE QUAYSIDE AT CANNOBIO.

church of the Madonna del Sasso, which can be reached in a short hour's climb or in seven minutes on the funicular railway. It contains some good pictures, notably a *Flight into Egypt* by Bramantino and a *Descent from the Cross* by Ciseri. A famous pilgrimage is made to it annually.

To explore the northern part of the lake one can follow the roads which skirt its shores. It is better, however, in this narrow fiord-like

THE CASTLES OF CANNERO.

SANTA CATERINA DEL SASSO NEAR LAVENO.

THE LAKE AT PALLANZA.

THE VILLA SAN REMIGIO, PALLANZA.

stretch to make use of one of the boats that ply between the scattered lakeside villages.

Departing from Locarno one gets a magnificent glimpse of the town and of the green hills that surround it, strewn with the white specks of country houses and hamlets. The boat rounds the delta which the Maggia is gradually making, stops at the little harbour of Magadino sprawled around the mouth of the Ticino, then at Brissago on the opposite shore, beautifully situated amongst gardens and very picturesque with its church on a terrace planted with ancient cypresses. At the head of a lovely valley very near Brissago, rises a Sacro Monte with

68

a church and fourteen shrines dating from the eighteenth century.

After leaving Brissago one enters Italy. The western shore belongs administratively to Piedmont, the eastern shore to Lombardy, and the centre of the lake is the boundary between the two regions. But because of the hump between Pallanza and Stresa, Piedmont can claim the glory of owning the most important and richest part of Lake Maggiore.

The first boat-stop in Italian territory is at Cannobio, a pleasant industrial town, very proud of its church, the Madonna della Pietà which the Government has classified as a National Monument, the equivalent of our Scheduled Ancient Monuments. It is a building of the early Renaissance, in the style of Bramante, with a dome by Pellegrino Tibaldi, that fine sixteenth-century Bolognese architect, who had the honour to be named in a famous poem in which Agostino Carracci stated the method — I almost said gave the recipe — for making a perfect picture : by borrowing the best quality that each great master had to offer. One must take from Tibaldi " the art of solid proportions ". Certainly those of

" BOY FISHING " BY GEMITO IN THE GARDENS OF THE VILLA TARANTO, PALLANZA.

69

the dome of Cannobio church are extremely successful. Unfortunately the interior of the vault is marred by an excess of stucco and decorations. One thinks quite naturally of Rome's worst Baroque churches. What a wealth of statues on vaults and ceilings ! Two angels hang over the choir, arms and legs extended, ready to fall. The church has an excellent altar-piece painted on wood in 1525, by Gaudenzio Ferrari, for the altar which it still adorns : *Christ Bearing the Cross*. The composition is good, the colour scheme warm, the scene animated ; yet there broods over it a dignified solemnity. I admire most the swooning Virgin in the foreground and the splendid heads lavishly praised by Burckhardt, who declares this work to be " the Piedmontese artist's finest altar picture ".

We are, incidentally, in a region rich in famous painters, for Luini was born here. Indeed, Luino — which we shall shortly visit after stopping at Maccagno — claims the honour of having been his birthplace, although unable to produce definite and reliable proofs. In this book we shall come upon many examples of this great artist's work.

Although it takes us a little distance from Lake Maggiore, a detour easily made in a car provides an opportunity to see the frescoes of Masolino da Panicale in the Collegiata at Castiglione Olona. Cardinal Castiglioni summoned the Umbrian painter to decorate the basilica which he had had built in 1421. With Masolino Tuscan art penetrated into northern Italy 50 years before the birth of Leonardo in Milan. " Castiglione, Olona, " declared Corrado Ricci, " is an oasis of Tuscan art in Lombardy ."

It is very interesting to compare Masolino's frescoes with those of Luini, which I shall discuss in connection with Lugano, and of Gaudenzio Ferrari who, alone, resisted the thraldom of da Vinci and succeeded in retaining his native originality — that of a realist born and bred among mountains. One could say that Lombardic art died with his death in 1546.

From Luino the boat re-crosses the lake and touches at Cannero beautifully sited and surrounded by olives, vines and orchards on the slope of Monte Carza. The shore, thickly populated here, has a very mild climate and oranges and lemons flourish in the open air. A picturesque touch to the landscape is added by two sadly ruined castles, the Castelli di Cannero. In the fifteenth century they served as a hideout for the five Mazzarda brothers, local brigands who held all the lakeside dwellers to ransom and resisted, for over two years, the four hundred men sent by Duke Filippo Visconti to put an end to their misdeeds.

The boat plies across the lake once more to Oggebio, built in a

AT PALLANZA.

AT STRESA.

BESIDE THE LAKE AT STRESA.

THE ISOLA DEI PESCATORI AND THE ISOLA MADRE, WITH PALLANZA IN THE BACKGROUND.

LAKE MAGGIORE AND THE ISOLA BELLA.

NEAR STRESA.

series of terraces on the slopes of hills covered with chestnut trees, then crosses back to call at Porto Valtravaglia, of the noble cypresses, and Laveno, an unremarkable industrial town though magnificently situated opposite the Borromean Islands, Monte Mottarone and Monte Rosa. Laveno is the point of departure for the convent of Santa Caterina and for the Sasso di Ferro which, at 3,980 feet, is not the highest but is certainly the finest of the summits overlooking the lake. From the top one sees a vast circular panorama extending over the Alps and the Plain

TERRACED GARDENS OF THE PALAZZO BORROMEO ON THE ISOLA BELLA.

GARDENS BESIDE THE LAKE ON THE ISOLA BELLA.

of Lombardy as far as Milan, whose cathedral steeple can be discerned on a clear day.

Opposite Laveno the whole wonderful stretch of the lake is spread before one : the Punta d'Intra, the emerald-coloured gulf where the Borromean Islands rise, the flower-grown shores of Pallanza and Stresa. Even those who share my preference for Lake Como to Lake Maggiore must admit that this grouping of elements is unsurpassed. Nowhere save at Bellagio can one see at one glance so many beautiful gardens with their green lushness reflected in the water.

There is no doubt that the Italians have at all times had a genius for gardening and terrace-building. When the countryside did not already consist of gardens, they created them, as they have done on the Isola Bella. It is noteworthy that the majority of the famous Italian gardens, and especially those which beautify these shores, are constructed in terraces on the hills. In France, on the other hand, the parks of the Ile de France or of Touraine extend over vast flat or very gently undulating plains : their lines stretch out to create a majestic harmony, coldly austere like Racine's verse or Bossuct's oratory. The gardens here in Italy have a more tortuous appearance, with sudden unexpected turnings, alternately sunny and shady corners, stairs, vases, balustrades and statues scattered about in great profusion. Evergreen trees such as pines, ilexes and cypresses complete the scenery of these lake-mirrored gardens. The cypresses, above all, add a touch of solemnity which compensates any tendency to over-prettiness and affectation that might otherwise mar the design. They always save the landscape from insipidity.

Of all the villas that adorn the shore between Pallanza and Intra, the most beautiful is the Villa San Remigio, unjustly neglected because of the formidable rivalry of the nearby Borromean Islands. The sight of it always fills me with real delight. In my opinion the art of Italian garden design has never been carried so far. It consists of nothing but terraces, statues, paths of clipped shrubs, great ornamental groves, columns, marble fountains, staircases with vases and splendid balustrades. And how superbly situated on a sort of promontory, called the Castagnola because of the age-old chestnut trees that overshadow it ! From the paths framed in luxuriant vegetation one overlooks first one side of the lake, then the other. There are huge clumps of rhododendrons and azaleas, almost as tall and lusty as those of the Villa Carlotta on the shores of Lake Como. And on each of the terraces rising in tiers above the house are masses of flowers, exhaling dense clouds of perfume, especially in the late afternoon. Purple sages glow like burning bushes in the sun's oblique rays. Great red and yellow cannas, gladioli of all colours, nod on the ends of their tall stalks. In the sunniest, most sheltered

IN THE GARDENS OF THE ISOLA BELLA.

corners oleanders, orange trees, palm trees strike their more fiery notes. One gratefully appreciates the cooler air in the shade of those skilfully pruned tall shrubs which, in springtime, give out their bitter-sweet odour.

Right next to the Villa San Remigio are the magnificent gardens of the Villa Taranto, created by Captain Neil McEacharn, a typical English park in an Italian setting. Lawns laid out at great expense, acres of rare flowers, clumps of lilies, lotuses, beds of water-lilies and aquatic plants, and rose arbours are scattered in skilful confusion among

A VIEW OF THE LAKE THROUGH A GRILLE ON THE ISOLA BELLA.

A KASHMIR CYPRESS ON THE ISOLA MADRE.

the green swards;
the tones and
colours are con-
trasted with great
ingenuity. The
only fault with
these gardens is
that they are not
right at the edge
of the lake,
which can only
be glimpsed
through the flow-
er clumps.

Opposite
Pallanza are two
towns popular
with tourists en-
tering Italy by the
Simplon route,
Baveno and
Stresa. The ho-
tels, established
at the very edge
of the lake, often
with a private
beach and land-
ing stage, are
among the most
pleasant I know,
especially for a
long stay. At
Baveno one can
see the parish
church of Santi
Gervasio e Prota-
sio, which dates

AN IRON GATE ON
THE ISOLA MADRE.

83

DRYING FISHING NETS ON THE ISOLA DEI PESCATORI.

DRYING FISH ON THE ISOLA DEI PESCATORI.

from the eleventh and twelfth centuries and parts of which are still in the Romanesque style despite unfortunate restorations. In the dome of the nearby baptistery, which also dates from the twelfth century, are some interesting frescoes. There are some beautiful villas on the terraced hillsides overlooking Baveno. The most famous is the Villa Branca, built in the English style, alien to these shores. It is proud of its garden and even prouder of the fact that Queen Victoria stayed there in 1879.

85

Stresa, officially called Stresa Borromeo, likewise comprises every kind of hotel, sumptuous and otherwise, sprawled along the quaysides and over the slopes of Monte Mottarone. On the Belgirate road the Villa Pallavicini and the Villa Vignolo are worth visiting : the latter, in particular, has some marvellous gardens, but it is very hard to gain admission. One can also see the Villa Ducale, where Antonio Rosmini died in 1855; and the famous and ideally situated Collegio Rosmini, in which the souvenirs of the philosopher are kept. He lies in the nearby church in a tomb with a monument by Vela.

A great many tourists are tempted, and very rightly, to climb Monte Mottarone. It is essential to go right to the summit (4890 feet) in order to see and enjoy one of the widest panoramas in the district. One discovers the vast circle of the Alps from Monte Viso right round to the Adamello massif. The view of the Monte Rosa chain is particularly beautiful. Southwards one looks right across the Plain of Lombardy where no less than seven lakes (Orta, Mergozzo, Maggiore, Biandronno, Varese, Monate and Comabbio) can be discerned scattered about. In clear weather the dome of Milan Cathedral and the Campanile of San Gaudenzio at Novara are easily visible.

One could visit other villas, but none of them can compete with the allure of the Borromean Islands.

It is a fact that the famous gardens of the Isola Bella often evoke a sense of disenchantment. Nature has been violated and perverted too much, here : man has not been content to use a terraced landscape, but has created it at all points and has piled up thereon so many marbles, vases and statues that the whole thing resembles a theatre set rather than a park. And yet having made this criticism, I admit that the gardens are wonderful, with their exotic flora : this includes coffee, cinnamon and tulip trees, coconut palms and enormous cedars of Lebanon and the Himalayas. Around these is a profusion of those shrubs which flourish vigorously here : the myrtles, azaleas, rhododendrons as large as trees, the immense oleanders overloaded with flowers and the fragrant groves of scented oleas. Throughout September their intoxicating odour hovers like everlasting incense over the lakes.

Beside the gardens stands the palazzo which was built for Conte Vitaliano Borromeo in the mid-seventeenth century, but was never finally completed. It contains luxuriously appointed salons, a bedroom where Napoleon slept, a little gallery of paintings where I especially

ON THE ISOLA DEI PESCATORI.

ON THE SLOPES OF MONTE MOTTARONE.

noticed two portraits by Boltraffio and by Luca Giordano and a chapel with three tombs carved by Amadeo and Bambaia.

This Vitaliano Borromeo was a great nobleman much taken with Platonic ideas. He liked ostentation and decided to create, on the hitherto arid soil of the Borromean Islands, the enchanted scene which is still admired there today. On the gardens, in particular, he spared no expense. For months on end, countless boats carried tons of fertile loam with which to make the terraces. And from every corner of Europe, and even from other parts of the world, the rarest plants and species were collected.

In the mellow atmosphere of the lake, even milder than that of the Lombardy Plain, a lush vegetation covered the gardens of the Isola Madre and grew rapidly more luxuriant each year. The park still retains a touch of wildness, restful to the eye : everything seems to grow more easily here than on the Isola Bella. One can enjoy here the cool freshness of real shade. There are terraces, too, though less obviously contrived. An uninhabited palazzo on the last one enjoys a superb view. This is, indeed, the centre of the panorama, in the middle of the lake and of the circle of mountains enclosing it, and close enough to the land to reveal in detail the shores of the incomparable bay. On one side lies Pallanza, a true pleasure resort, cluttered with hotels, villas, gardens ; and on the other, Baveno and Stresa, on equally magnificent sites. And everywhere, beside the roads that twist and turn along the lake's edge is an unbroken succession of houses and parks, to enumerate which would be positively tedious. This is the view which Stendhal considered a perfect pair with that of the bay of Naples : he even declared it to be " more moving ".

Less magnificent but more picturesque and enchanting is the tiny Isola dei Pescatori, entirely covered with houses packed suffocatingly close together. The streets are quite absurdly narrow. The three hundred or so inhabitants occupy — I don't know how — a space so restricted that they live as it were in each other's pockets. Few corners of Italy are so utterly Italian. At the north-western end of the island is a little esplanade planted with lime and plane trees festooned with fishing nets. This is the inhabitants' only promenade and it juts out into the lake like a ship's prow. From the point there is a beautiful view over Baveno and its hills. Unfortunately an enormous quarry makes an ugly scar here. Further back stands Monte Orfano, with the Corni di Nibbio still further away. There are more marble quarries here, those from which the marble was obtained for the building of the dome of Milan Cathedral but being less visible these do not mar the landscape so much.

At the other end of the island, the arbours of an inn are mirrored in the lake. I remembered having visited it previously, but I had no inkling of the welcome that was awaiting me this year. At first I could not understand the reason for it : I had forgotten a sentence I had written earlier, which was now pointed out to me in a copy of the first edition of this same book, *The Italian Lakes*. I was assured that it had brought many customers to the delightful inn. " What a delicious meal one can have ," I had written, " at the old *Trattoria del Verbano*, when one is familiar with and enjoys Milanese cooking ! " This was flattery pleasing to the vanity that lurks in the breast of every author. And once again, as forty years ago beside the lake, I relished excellent Italian cooking.

BELGIRATE.

THE CASTLE OF ANGERA, FROM ARONA.

I shall not risk ridicule by comparing it with French cooking : but to the sensible gourmet it can provide a feast. Obviously one must not demand, as my ignorant countrymen often do, lobsters, oysters, lamb chops, grilled steak or roast chicken : one must be prepared to accept the local produce. The wines lack the excellence of some of our vineyards but they are very good and nearly always reasonable. A bottle of Barolo or a flask of real Chianti is better than a dubious Beaujolais...

And what more delightful setting for an autumnal lunch than the lake glittering in the sunshine between the Isola Madre and the Isola Bella with Laveno and the Sasso del Ferro in the background and, still more distant, the round dome of the Campo dei Fiori above Varese !

●

The southern part of the lake is less interesting : compared with those we are reluctantly leaving, the shores are too flat and there is less picturesque detail. Nevertheless there are still many opulent buildings, almost all owned by Milanese families.

On the western shore the boat stops in turn at Belgirate and at Lesa, which form one continuous township, and at Meina — where, among many beautiful villas, one must point out the Villa Faraggiana which has a magnificent garden.

Then across the lake to stop at Angera, dominated by its massive castle, built by the Visconti family and owned by the Borromeo family since 1489.

The final stop is at Arona, an old town built at the foot of a sort of sheer cliff crowned by ruins. This acquired a sudden prosperity when it became the focal point of the railway lines from the Simplon, Genoa and Turin. It would be a mistake for travellers to neglect to visit the church of the Santi Martyri, which houses many fine works, notably an altar-piece by Bergognone; and more especially the collegiate church of Santa Maria, where one can admire a polyptych by Gaudenzio Ferrari dated 1511. But they too often neglect these buildings and artifacts in favour of the gigantic statue of San Carlo Borromeo standing on a hill just outside the town, which forms an irresistible attraction. This monument, one of the largest in existence, 65 feet in height, with a pedestal which adds a further 40 feet, was erected in honour of Conte Carlo Borromeo, born at Arona in 1538, who became Abbot at the age of twelve and Cardinal-Archbishop of Milan at twenty-two. But he deserved these exceptional honours. He exerted a stern discipline over his clergy and gave proof of the most heroic devotion during the Plague of 1610. The statue is quite second-rate. Let us leave the tourists struggling to ascend painfully, at a snail's pace, the staircase leading to the enormous head, whilst we walk down to the lake to enjoy the play of the bright sunlight on the water.

OLEANDERS IN FRONT OF THE ALBERGO VERBANO ON THE ISOLA DEI PESCATORI.

MONTE SAN SALVATORE, LAKE LUGANO.

ON LAKE LUGANO.

CHAPTER FOUR

LAKE LUGANO

Lake Lugano — or *Lacus Ceresio*, to give it its Latin name — situated between Lake Maggiore and Lake Como, which are exclusively Italian, apart from the northern end of Maggiore, belongs on the contrary almost entirely to Switzerland. The only parts which are Italian are the tip of the Porlezza arm, the little enclave of Campione and the western shore from Ponte Tresa to Porto Ceresio. Moreover its general conformation and tortuous shape are reminiscent of the Swiss lakes, especially of Lake Lucerne.

Its appearance is most frequently wild and Alpine. Only the bay of Lugano, its central portion, can compete in smiling graciousness and beauty with its great neighbours.

Many streams pour into Lake Lugano. The Tresa, its outlet at the end of the western arm, flows into Lake Maggiore.

The rugged, almost uninhabited banks skirting the Capologo arm and those of Porto Ceresio and Ponte Tresa will not interest hurrying travellers. But one must exclude Morcote, delightfully situated at the end of the peninsula formed by Monte San Salvatore, with terraced vineyards rising above it on the slope of Monte Arbostora. This village's arcaded houses stretch alongside the lake, and a staircase with a hundred steps leads up to the Madonna del Sasso, an ancient church in which some remarkable early sixteenth-century frescoes, partly the work of the school of Leonardo, are preserved. Beside it stand a campanile and the cypresses of a most romantic cemetery. These elements compose a truly exquisite picture : unfortunately it has been somewhat vulgarized by reproductions.

The loveliest stretch of the lake is the basin between Porlezza at the far north-eastern end and the long railway bridge which cuts the lake in two so awkwardly between Melide and Bissone : though, to be still more precise, only the northern slope of this basin is lovely.

Almost the whole of the southern shore, indeed, is wild. Only the little corner round Campione seems anxious to justify by its smiling, colourful appearance its status of an Italian enclave. Tourists come here far more for its elegant casino, where the gaming tables flourish, than to make a pilgrimage to the birthplace of the " Maestri Campionesi ", those famous sculptors and architects who, in the fourteenth century, were the chief master masons of Milan Cathedral. If one has an hour to spare one might visit the oratory of San Pietro, dating from 1326, and the parish church, rich in works of art.

The shore between Porlezza and Lugano, exposed to the sun and sheltered by the mountains from the cold winds, recalls parts of Lake Maggiore. First comes Cima, its church surmounting a terrace and surrounded by four sentinel cypresses : a fine decorative pattern; then San Mamete, overlooked by the village of Castello; and finally Oria, very proud of its villa where Fogazzaro used to spend the autumn.

The entry into Switzerland is heralded only by the visit of the customs official, for the village of Gandria is completely Italian in character. Backed by the foot of Monte Bré, its terraces almost sheer above the

ORIA.

MONTE BRÉ AND THE PORLEZZA ARM OF THE LAKE SEEN FROM THE PARADISO.

lake, its arcaded houses seem to be built on top of one another in a confused mass of roofs and tiny gardens shaded by oleanders and trellises.

We may note, on the opposite shore, the village of Santa Margherita, much less gay because it faces north. The funicular railway climbs 2950 feet from here to Lanzo d'Intelvi. This village, situated on a smiling plateau, is much sought after as a rural retreat in the summer by the people of Milan.

●

After Gandria the boat rounds the Punta della Castagnola, dotted uniformly with villas and gardens, and enters the bay of Lugano, one of the most magnificent bays on any lake in Europe. The mountains that overhang it greatly enhance its grandeur. Some of these are sufficiently striking in profile to have moved Chateaubriand to make a startling comparison : " The mountains surrounding Lake Lugano, " he declared, " the feet of which touch one another only at the level of the lake, resemble islands separated by narrow channels. Their graceful green-clad shapes remind me of the Azores archipelago. " From their disorderly summits there are splendid views over the Alps, the lakes and the Lombardy Plain.

Few countries possess so many funicular railways : from Lugano alone one can count four : those of San Salvatore, of Monte Generoso, of Lanzo d'Intelvi and of Monte Bré.

These mountains make a marvellous frame for the town of Lugano : stretching in a curve for several miles along the edge of the lake, it is justly styled the " Queen of Ceresio " by the lakeside residents. With its twenty thousand inhabitants it is the largest and finest town in the Ticino (especially if the surrounding villages are added, making an aggregate of twenty-nine thousand). Almost equidistant from Lake Como and from Lake Maggiore, there is no pleasanter or more suitable spot for the tourist to stay in if he wishes to visit the three lakes at his leisure. It provides the advantages and amenities of a town with the additional pleasure of being able to leave it at any moment on one of the many boats that ply in all directions across the lake. There is no better place for a stroll than beneath the arcades flanking the old streets and, still more pleasant, on the wide pavements of the quay that runs for several miles beside the lake from the Punta della Castagnola right to the Paradiso. Gabriel Fauré, who visited Lugano during many summers and composed his *Pénélope* there, was very fond of this promenade : we used often to walk together there in those happy years

GANDRIA.

before the first war, when one could enjoy life fully and work with no other preoccupation than Art and Beauty.   Those hours beneath Lugano's shady trees and beside the lake, those trips to San Salvatore and the expeditions towards Menaggio and Lake Como, to Bellagio and the Villa Carlotta remain among the happiest memories of my life. But of the dozen friends who once gathered around the " last enchanter ", as I have called him, how many can now share my memories ?   Only Marguerite Long and René Fauchois to my knowledge.   How moving I find the photos that recall some of those moments...

At the end of the winter the scenery is still more wonderful. I remember my amazement one day when, arriving straight from Paris in early March to give a lecture, I disembarked at Lugano. The first spring flowers were opening in the gardens. The Australian magnolias were smothered in their supple pink petals. At the head of the Bay of Porlezza the white pyramid of Monte Legnone was surrounded by green mountains. Beside Monte Bré the Boglia was covered with snow. And above the rooftops of the town were silhouetted the summits overhanging Locarno and the northern shores of Lake Maggiore.

Few landscapes are so varied as those one sees as one follows the quayside of Lugano towards the Punta della Castagnola or towards the Paradiso. One might almost say they change at every step. The views are equally fine from the terrace of the station, or of that in front of the church of San Lorenzo with its charming early Renaissance marble façade and three most interesting portals.

Lugano is proud of the monuments carved by a local nineteenth-century sculptor, Vincenzo Vela, a native of Mendrisio who specialized in funerary statues which are to be found in nearly all the lakeside cemeteries. The most famous is the *Desolation* in the Villa Ciani at the end of the quay near the mouth of the Cassarate. This was erected by the two Ciani brothers in memory of their mother who died in Milan while they were in enforced exile in Switzerland during the revolution. The museum of local history was recently installed in this Villa Ciani. It contains objects found during excavations, local costumes, furniture and reconstructions of Ticinese domestic interiors.

●

Lugano's artistic glory is linked with Bernardino Luini : he has left two of his most beautiful works in Santa Maria degli Angeli, whose

THE VIRGIN AND CHILD WITH ST JOHN BY BERNARDINO LUINI
IN SANTA MARIA DEGLI ANGELI AT LUGANO.

mean façade on the quayside skirting the lake gives one no idea of the marvels within. Those who are unaware of them never dream of entering the church. How could one suspect one's nearness to some superb frescoes by Luini, the good Luini whose charming and melodious name seems to evoke the poetry and peacefulness of the lakes on whose shores the artist was born, worked and died ?

This church of Lugano is one of those sanctuaries, of which I am most fond, wherein one finds the very spirit of an artist concealed behind an insignificant, mediocre exterior. For four centuries it has remained virtually unchanged ; quite close to the cosmopolitan crowd that fills the hotels one can spend long hours uninterrupted by either tourists or guides.

Unless one makes a pilgrimage to Saronno, where most of Luini's works now remain, one cannot come to know this artist save by studying the frescoes at Lugano. For he is first and foremost a *frescante*. Those who judge him only by his easel paintings cannot appreciate the

A DETAIL OF BERNARDINO LUINI'S CRUCIFIXION, WITH THE MAGDALEN
IN THE FOREGROUND, IN SANTA MARIA DEGLI ANGELI, LUGANO.

THE PORLEZZA ARM OF LA

M MONTE SAN SALVATORE.

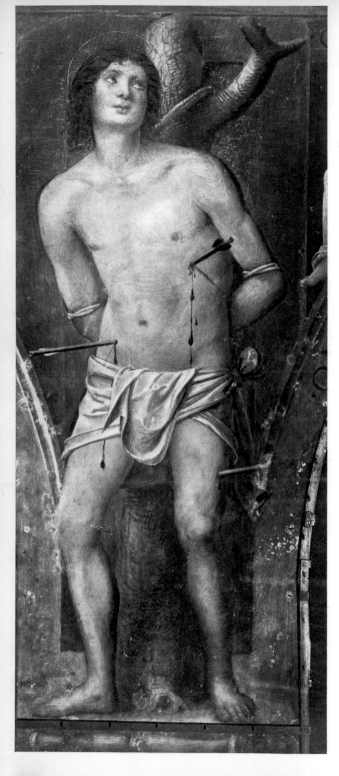

artist's true genius : he had no room in so restricted a space to pour out his ardent, tender, enthusiastic and spontaneous spirit. In the much larger area of the fresco, on the other hand, he could spread the work out to his liking. Unhampered by time or by the exigencies of a definite programme, he obeyed no other law than his own fancy. He put his whole personality into the work, with all his virtues and shortcomings.

One can form one's own opinion of that on this wall where he painted his largest composition. All the episodes of the *Passion* are depicted here, with over one hundred and fifty *dramatis personae*. The composition is rather cold and one can sense the pains Luini took in planning so theatrical and so complex a layout. But the details are delightful and there are few figures more moving than the pathetic portrait of St John making his vow to the dying Christ ; or that of the Magdalen kneeling at the foot of the Cross, smiling ecstatically beneath her long golden tresses.

SAINT SEBASTIAN
BY BERNARDINO LUINI IN SANTA
MARIA DEGLI ANGELI, LUGANO.

Admittedly on examining this fresco more carefully I discern some confused groups, some inexpressive faces and some false perspectives. But the impression of the whole composition is fascinating. There are so many pleasing tones, so skilfully graduated, so much mellowness and softness everywhere, that I would not dream of further criticism. I am captivated, just as I am by music which grips me from the first few bars immediately I hear them, even though I recognize its failings and its mediocrity. I no longer notice the faults. My attention is held only by those exquisite details which Luini has poured out more prodigally here than anywhere else.

And then there is that delightful little lunette of the *Virgin, the Infant Jesus and St John the Baptist* in the first right-hand chapel. Once situated above the door between the cloister and the refectory, this was moved into the church when the cloister was pulled down to make way for the great mansion now standing there. Burckhardt says that this " is of a beauty worthy

SAINT ROCH
BY BERNARDINO LUINI IN SANTA MARIA DEGLI ANGELI, LUGANO.

109

of Leonardo ". It was, incidentally, in separate figures such as these, doing nothing in particular, that Luini excelled. And I am sure that I would give the whole vast fresco of the *Passion* for this lunette.

The painter found peace and joy in this convent of Lugano — for such it was when he worked there — just as he did earlier in the sanctuary at Saronno. He was never so happy elsewhere as in the calm retreat of the cloister. Here — no doubt for a minute sum, but freed from all material cares — he could devote himself wholeheartedly to the enchanted profession, that which he called the *mirabile e clarissima arte di pittura*. He worked many months in this convent of Lugano, where he apparently stayed for long periods, and where, after four centuries, something of his dreaming spirit still hovers.

His female figures are as graceful and as beautiful as the girls of Lombardy, with opulent forms, languorous eyes, and pink cheeks, yielding to the touch, one imagines, like the flesh of ripe fruit. He was equally adept at depicting every type of masculine beauty. This also one can discover convincingly in this church at Lugano, merely by studying the two beautiful figures of saints which he painted below the large fresco.

The *St Sebastian* shows that he had a complete mastery of nude painting. In the *St Roch* on the other hand, one admires the tremendous concentration of vitality and thought which gives such intense poignancy to the face.

In Luini's frescoes one is far less aware of the influence Leonardo da Vinci exercised over him than in his easel pictures. He strove to free himself from it especially when working in solitude, in the depths of a village or convent church, under the cloister arcades. And yet even here one finds evidence of his admiration for the great Florentine. On the left partition wall is an excellent copy of Leonardo's *Last Supper* which he painted for the convent refectory, and which was placed here when that building was pulled down.

I am perpetually amazed that Stendhal should have regretted that " no great painter had immortalized " the beauty of Lombardy. He was forgetting Luini, who perfectly expressed that beauty which Manzoni described as " *molle a un tratto e maestosa* " — gentle and yet vigorous at the same time. He was also forgetting Leonardo, who felt the attraction of Lombardy, of its women and its youths ; but he expressed their charm with that elegant refinement which is the essence of the Florentine spirit. The flowers on the tree of art burst forth at every level : those of Luini, very close to the earth, are within reach of our hands : we can easily gather them and inhale their perfume.

The reader will forgive me for lingering a little in this church of Lugano. But we shall not again have the opportunity to encounter so important a group of paintings anywhere else on the Italian Lakes.

THE LAKESIDE.

VARENNA.

WROUGHT-IRON GATE OF THE VILLA CARLOTTA.

CHAPTER FIVE

LAKE COMO

This is the loveliest of the lakes. If Lake Maggiore is superior in both size and grandeur it cannot — save in the bay around the Borromean Islands — compare with it in charm, general harmony and colour. It has a more sheltered situation, especially in the Como arm, and a more southern type of vegetation. One might describe it as the most Italian of the Lombardy lakes — not only because it is situated completely in Italian territory, but because it offers us lavishly all the magnificence and all the charm that the name Italy immediately evokes in our imagination.

From earliest times writers have sung of *Lacus Larius*. Already

THE NORTH DOORWAY OF COMO CATHEDRAL, " PORTA DELLA RANA ".

THE BROLETTO AND THE FAÇADE OF THE CATHEDRAL AT COMO.

Cassiodorus was declaring
it *ad solas delicias instituto*
and Pliny the Younger,
who owned several coun-
try residences around its
flower-decked shores, was
constantly complaining
whenever his affairs kept
him away from them, in
Rome or elsewhere. In
modern times, it con-
tinues to arouse the en-
thusiasm of artists, novel-
ists and poets. Shelley
declared : " The beauty of
this lake surpasses everything I have seen
hitherto. " It is the
inspiration of some of
Stendhal's pleasantest
pages : many scenes
in his *Chartreuse de
Parme* were set on its
shores; and Manzoni also
makes his *Promessi Sposi*
walk its banks. At the
risk of seeming to lack
modesty, I recall the
impression it made on
me as a young writer,
when I saw it for the first
time.

It was at Bellagio
that I began to write
*Amour sous les lauriers-
roses*, the voluptuous

STATUE OF PLINY THE
YOUNGER ON THE FAÇADE
OF COMO CATHEDRAL.

A DETAIL FROM BERNARDINO LUINI'S ADORATION OF THE MAGI IN COMO CATHEDRAL.

TORNO AND THE CAMPANILE OF THE CHURCH OF SANTA TECLA.

LAKE COMO FROM THE PUNTA DI TORNO.

scenes of which took place in the setting of the Villa Serbelloni.

Indeed, the human spirit cannot possibly imagine anything more gracious, more soothing to the eye than this emerald chalice set like a jewel in a ring of splendid hills, dominated by the snow-capped Alpine summits to the north. And how endless the variety of shapes and colours on its shores, where olive and chestnut, mulberry and walnut trees grow side by side, with forests higher up the slopes, villages on the hillsides or at the water's edge, chapels, castles—more or less ruined, villas surrounded by gardens, and magnificent parks !

●

IN TORNO HARBOUR.

SPRING IN TORNO.

The Lake of Como is shaped like an inverted Y and divided into three arms — the northern arm, the arm of Lecco and that of Como itself, which is by far the most remarkable. It is thirty-one miles long and only two and a half miles across at its widest point, between Menaggio and Varenna. The many promontories even make it seem like a string of small lakes and if they occasionally obstruct the view of the whole lake they add to the picturesqueness of each fresh panorama. Its two main tributaries are the rivers Mera and Adda which bring in the waters from the Alpine mountain groups that slope towards it. Its only outlet, the Adda, flows out to the south-east, from the southern tip of the Lecco arm.

Let us make a complete circuit of the lake, starting from Como, which is worth a long visit. Como is a beautiful town of 72,000 inhabitants and is by far the most important of all the towns situated on the lakes. Tourists, attracted by the water and anxious to embark, too often neglect it and hardly pause to give it a glance. I recall that previously I did likewise and even, following Maurice Barrès' lead, mocked Taine who, in his *Voyage en Italie*, devoted more pages to Como's cathedral than to the shores of the lake itself. For had he not started by rejoicing in the idea that he was about to discover beautiful landscapes ? " After three months spent in front of paintings and statues, one is like a man

THE VILLA PLINIANA.

A VIEW OF LAKE COMO FROM MOLINA CEMETERY.

who has dined in town every night for three months : give me bread, not pineapples ! One climbs lightheartedly into the train, knowing that on reaching one's destination one will find lakes, trees, real mountains, that the landscapes will no longer be a mere three feet long, no longer be enclosed within narrow gilt frames... " But next day, having toured the lake without leaving the boat, he devotes a brief page to the

THE VILLA D'ESTE AT CERNOBBIO.

THE ENTRANCE TO THE VILLA PIZZO.

wonders he has been feasting his eyes on, and which he had apparently longed for so passionately! And then he succumbs to the temptation of visiting the Duomo and writes a long chapter about the mixture of Italian and Gothic amongst the artistic works of the Renaissance.

After a careful study of this cathedral at Como I understand our philosopher's enthusiasm and cannot too strongly advise the traveller

THE CHAPEL OF SANTA AGATA AT MOLTRASIO, LAKE COMO.

BRIENNO.

to devote at least a few hours to it. Even after seeing Italian towns abounding in works of art he will find that it contains much to claim and hold his attention.

The façade of this cathedral, with its three divisions emphasized by vertical bands of statues one above the other, is extremely original. The central portion is particularly skilfully wrought and very richly decorated. The central doorway, surmounted by a row of five tall figures and by a rose window surrounded by niches, is flanked on either

AT ARGEGNO.

THE VILLA ARCONATI AT THE PUNTA DI BALBIANELLO.

side by elegant slender windows, beneath which are the celebrated statues of Pliny the Elder and Pliny the Younger. I observe also that there is an abundance of statues everywhere. The windows themselves are bordered with them. One might count pretty well a hundred on this façade, though at first sight it appears to be almost plain because of its large flat areas. The architectural details are sometimes Gothic, sometimes Renaissance. Rarely can one see embodied in marble a better example of the conflict of forces that divided the fifteenth century. These transitional works have, moreover a simplicity and emphatic vigour indicative of an art that was healthy and youthful. Undoubtedly certain naïvetés and a too-literal imitation of natural forms demonstrate that the spirit has not yet attained full mastery. An excess of clumsy invention is evident in the exaggerated curves, the unruly masses of hair. But this desire to portray and express life is, by its awkwardness, more attractive than many excessively clever and coldly perfect works. Moreover, Lombardic sculpture is chiefly ornamental and its sole purpose is to contribute to the harmonious effect of the whole work. The artists are decorators rather than statue-makers.

One can better appreciate this by studying the doors on either side of the cathedral : the south door seems clearly to bear the mark of Bramante :

THE ISOLA COMACINA.

LAKE COMO AT LENNO.

VIEW OF TREMEZZO FROM A LANDING-STAGE AT BOLVEDRO.

the breadth of design, the restraint in handling details, the firmness of line, the nobility of the composition are worthy of the great architect. One has only to see the other door to realize what distinguishes a master from his imitators. The latter — sometimes called the Porta della Rana, because of a frog carved in one of the pillars — is the work of the Rodari brothers and one guesses that these two Lombardic artists were determined to improve on the model which served as their inspiration : they have succeeded only in making it richer and more complicated — excessively so.   Why else those figures on the entablature, and that niche surmounted in its turn by statues ?

Why these enormous columns carved and loaded with ornament like altar pillars ?   I see here the work of the same hands and minds that wrought the Duomo at Milan and the Carthusian monastery at Pavia.

But I must not do what I censured Taine for doing.   Let us turn

AZALEAS IN THE GARDEN OF THE VILLA CARLOTTA.

THE GARDEN OF THE VILLA CARLOTTA.

THE VILLA DEL SOLE, BOLVEDRO.

now to gaze upon the lake rippling gently in the limpid air this lovely morning, as Carducci has described it :

... palpito il lago di Virgilio, come velo di sposa,
che s'apre al bacio del promesso amore.

First we will traverse the eastern shore of the Como arm, the wildest and steepest bank, but not to be passed over on that account. Starting at the Piazza Cavour the road follows at first the shore. Then, beyond the station for the funicular railway that ascends to Brunate, it skirts a series of gardens and villas, some of which, like the Villa Margherita, are splendid. This spot seems to have been at all times the favourite of the great Italian actresses. One comes successively upon the Villa Capranica which belonged to La Ristori, the Villa Roccabruna on the site of the villa owned by Giuditta Pasta, the famous singer for whom Bellini composed *La Somnambula* and *Norma*, and finally the Villa Taglioni.

Seen from the boat, the village of Torno looks comparatively uninteresting. Yet it is very picturesque, with a series of alleys climbing from the water's edge towards the hillside. Here one can admire the Lombardic façade of the church of Santa Tecla, the west door of San Giovanni and the Campo Santo descending in steps, with fine views over the lake between the cypresses. Then the coast grows wilder and one observes the bright façade of the Villa Pliniana silhouetted against the dark mountain background. Framed in tall cypresses, the palace itself, where Napoleon, Ugo Foscolo and Rosmini stayed, is built on the site of a country residence owned by Pliny beside the source of an intermittent spring which greatly puzzled his imagination : in a letter to Licinius Sura on the subject, he enumerated all the explanations for this unusual phenomenon which seemed plausible at that time.

This is one of the grimmest spots on these usually pleasant shores, and one can readily appreciate that this unfriendly, almost mysterious, setting would have increased the awe and terror of the Ancients.

The road continues through a rugged lonely landscape, which is in sharp contrast to that of the opposite shore, covered with gardens and country houses. There are a few small towns, the most important being the picturesque village of Nesso rising in tiers up the mountainside, at the mouth of a small valley, and Lezzeno, level with the pretty Isola Comacina on the other bank. The road hugs the steep cliff of the Sassi Grosgalli whence there is a magnificent view over the Tremezzina. In the church at San Giovanni one can see a fine *Christ in Triumph* by Gaudenzio Ferrari. Suddenly the landscape becomes pleasant and fertile. We perceive the roofs and gardens of Bellagio, which we shall visit on another occasion, from another direction.

●

Let us now return to Como and follow the road which skirts the western side of the lake. Huge and sumptuous villas begin at the edge

137

of the town, and they continue without interruption. Unfortunately, as I earlier lamented, they are beginning to disappear among the many buildings of every kind now springing up on these shores. The most important is the Villa dell'Olmo, which belonged in turn to the Odescalchi and the Visconti families and is now the property of the Commune of Como and a public garden. It is very attractive but a trifle too solemn for my liking. It takes its name from the centuries-old elm trees standing in its forecourt. It has been classified as a National Monument because of its superb salons decorated with stucco, with frescoes by Appiani and bas-reliefs by Thorwaldsen.

The Villa d'Este at Cernobbio is even more magnificent and its transformation into a luxury hotel has in no way disfigured it. It was built in 1568 for Cardinal Tolomeo Gallio; in 1815 it became the property of Caroline of Brunswick and sheltered her deplorable love affairs. All the tourists who have sailed, or now sail, round the lake in a boat have admired, while passing Cernobbio, the splendid avenue of cypresses flanking a series of waterfalls, dominated, at the top, by a statue of Hercules.

The Villa Pizzo, on a promontory, belonged to the Archduke Renier of Austria. At the end of a tiny valley rising in terraces up the mountainside is the little holiday resort of Moltrasio which prides itself on the fact that the Catanian musician, Vincenzo Bellini, used to stay there. He spent several months in the Villa Salterio and the Villa Passalacqua where he composed parts of *La Somnambula*.

It would be boring and monotonous to try to describe all the villas which adorn the hamlets whose bright, gay colour-washed houses are strung out along the bank like the beads of a rosary : Urio, Carate, Laglio and Brienno. These are all delightfully situated, either close beside the water or else on a hillside, amid parks and gardens overhung with large clumps of oleanders.

Argegno at the mouth of the beautiful Intelvi river valley is more important. A road ascends the mountainside to the popular holiday resorts of Castiglione and San Fedele and on to Lanzo d'Intelvi. This village can be reached from the other side of the plateau by the funicular railway which starts at Santa Margherita on Lake Lugano.

After Argegno, the magical effect becomes still greater. The lakeside, growing ever more verdant and lush, forms a series of bays in which are situated little fishing villages that lie hidden among the trees : Colonno, Sala, Campo. Opposite these and separated from them by a narrow channel, is the tiny, completely green Isola Comacina, the

AT CADENABBIA.

lake's only island. This nevertheless played an historic and martial role in the Middle Ages when it was an impressive fortress. In 962 it was the refuge of Berengar II, King of Italy. Recent excavations have revealed some interesting archaeological remains. But the legend which claims that this tiny island was once a real city with nine churches and a castle is a slight exaggeration : the remains of only two buildings have been discovered. Today there is but a single church on it dedicated

to St John the Baptist, which is why it is also called Isola di San Giovanni. In 1917 it was bequeathed to Albert I of Belgium. He presented it to the Milan Academy of Fine Arts which turned it into a rest home for artists. The box-like buildings are studios for painters and sculptors.

In the village of Ospedaletto, next to Campo, stands the campanile which, as one of the curiosities of these shores, has been popularized on post-cards and photographs. This is a pretty eleventh-century building crowned by a Gothic bell-tower of the most pleasing appearance.

The road then cuts across the little peninsula called Punta di Balbianello, so picturesque from the boat as it rounds the point. At the end of the eighteenth century the beautiful Villa Arconati-Visconti was built here, with its elegant porticos,

MENAGGIO.

141

THE CASTLE, REZZONICO.

wreathed with greenery and flowers, facing in both directions over the lake, towards Como and towards Bellagio. Silvio Pellico was living here just before his arrest.

Next, in a sheltered spot which makes it a popular winter resort, comes Lenno. Its church of San Stefano, erected on the ruins of a

Roman temple, has an eleventh-century crypt. It was undoubtedly at Lenno that one of Pliny's two villas stood which he called respectively " Tragœdia " and " Comœdia ", because of their position, one high up, the other at the water's edge, " the one wearing buskins, the other lowly socks ". Some submerged shafts of columns and some capitals do prove that there used to be an important building at this spot. According to the best authority only this one villa would have been at Lenno : the Villa Tragœdia would have stood on the hill of Bellagio across the lake.

From Lenno a fairly arduous but interesting climb takes one to the summits of Monti Tremezzo (5576 feet), Galbiga (5570 feet) and Crocione (5283 feet). Although the lowest, the last provides the finest view over the whole lake and over the Brianza.

●

Beyond Lenno the really enchanting part of Lake Como begins, starting with the Tremezzina, a delightful region stretching in a ribbon beside the shore as far as Cadenabbia, where the villas stand so close together that they form one great uninterrupted park. The name " Garden of Lombardy " is sometimes given to this shore. Maurice Barrès took up this name and extended it to include the entire region of the Italian Lakes. In the centre of this region is the attractive village of Tremezzo built in terraces round a natural amphitheatre on the slope of Monte Crocione. Spring and autumn are delightful here and even the winters are very mild.

A row of very old plane trees with wide-spreading branches follows the shore right on to Cadenabbia. Opposite on the far bank is the exquisite landscape of Bellagio and the Serbelloni promontory. The villas continue without interruption along the road. The loveliest of all is the Villa Carlotta which, before the construction of the lakeside road, stretched right to the lake. A magnificent wrought-iron gateway now guards the entrance to this villa, built in the mid-eighteenth century for the Milanese nobleman Giorgio Clerici. Later it belonged to the Conti Sommariva. It was known to Stendhal as the Casa Sommariva and it is this which often crops up in La Chartreuse de Parme. In the middle of the last century it passed into the hands of Princess Albert of Prussia who presented it to her daughter Charlotte when she married the Duke of Saxe-Meiningen. It now belongs to the Italian Government.

The Villa Carlotta offers to visitors two marvels : first its garden in which the vegetation seems almost tropical in its vigour and abundance — where groves of camellias, cedars, magnolias, gigantic myrtles grow, where one walks between tall hedges of rhododendrons and azaleas, where grottoes of greenery and flowers provide astonishing glimpses over the sun-spangled lake, and where the perfumes are at times so heady as to be almost overwhelming. And then, at the entrance to the palace there is a room full of marbles by famous sculptors. I have never really liked the works by Canova in this collection, not even the copy of the *Cupid and Psyche* group, and yet this so excited Gustave Flaubert that he admits, in his travel notes, having embraced Psyche almost amorously. I like the works by Thorwaldsen but little better. But I do agree that his relief frieze of *The Triumph of Alexander* which runs right round the walls is splendidly decorative. This had been modelled in plaster by the sculptor in 1811 to the order of Napoleon, as decoration for the throne-room at the Quirinal; and it was carved in marble for the Conte Sommariva in 1828. I prefer a less frigid, youthful work of Thorwaldsen's, a *Triumph of Bacchus* which forms a chimney moulding in the billiard-room of this fine villa.

From Cadenabbia to Menaggio the shore is an unbroken succession of gardens and villas emulating one another in luxury and elegance. At Menaggio, after descending in wonderful hairpin-bends, the little railway and the new road linking the Lakes of Como and Lugano come to an end. Of no special interest to the tourist, it is both a busy commercial centre and an important place for routes at the mouth of the Val Menaggina. Being cool and breezy, its many hotels are very popular in summer.

After Menaggio the banks are less picturesque, with fewer splendid and beautiful residences. Nevertheless the many villages which occur at intervals beside the blue waters of the lake, like a string of topaz and coral beads, have great charm.

Here is a list of them, in succession : Loveno, with many villas, including the Villa Vigoni containing two Thorwaldsen bas-reliefs; Nobiallo, Acquaseria and Rezzonico, at the foot of its ancient cypress-girt castle whence came the family of Pope Clement XIII; Cremia opposite the cone-shaped Monte Legnone, with a hilltop church in which there are a *Virgin* by Bergognone and a *St Michael* attributed to Veronese; Musso, with its marble quarries and the ruins of an old fortress where Giovan-Giacopo de' Medici held out so long against the powerful Sforza family; and lastly Dongo — with the Stendhalian name — which, in the Middle Ages, with its two neighbours Gravedona and Sorico made

THE CLOISTER AT DONGO.

SANTA MARIA DEL TIGLIO, GRAVEDONA.

up the little state of the Three Priories, the " Tre Pievi ". This tiny but brave republic successfully confronted the forces of the Emperor Barbarossa in 1178 and was treated by the Emperor as an equal at the Treaty of Constance. Mussolini was captured near Dongo on April 27, 1945 while fleeing towards Germany, and the following day he was shot down, near Tremezzo.

This north-west side of the lake from Menaggio to Colico is quite busy, with cement and metallurgical factories, notably at Acquaseria and Dongo. But between these industrial oases the lakeside, with its fields full of meadow saffron in autumn, its alders and walnut trees, reminds one of parts of Dauphiné.

In a sense Gravedona closes the northern arm of the lake. Its impressive four-towered castle overlooks the water. This is the Palazzo del Frova built by Pellegrino Tibaldi for Cardinal Tolomeo Gallio, a perfect example of the princely villas of the late sixteenth century, with great open porticos in the centres of the two principal façades. One should certainly see two churches; first Santa Maria del Tiglio, a beautiful twelfth-century building, with three apses and a nave above which rises the campanile. Above the altar in one of these apses is a great crucifix with the cross and the body of Our Lord carved from a single block of wood. Next one should visit San Vincenzo, dating back many centuries : it was first restored in 1072. The crypt with its ponderous rough-hewn pillars contained valuable treasure which I saw previously, when preparing the first edition of this book, notably a superb silver cross, the work of a local craftsman, Gregorio da Gravedona. The treasure was stolen in 1920 and has been replaced by some fairly accurate copies.

●

We will neglect the few fishing villages in the marshes formed by deposits from the rivers Mera and Adda at the end of the lake and pass on to the eastern shore which we will now traverse, starting at Colico, quite an important terminus for the railway and the roads leading down from the Valtellina and the Engadine valleys.

From Colico almost as far as Lecco, road and railway skirt the edge of the lake side by side. And as the mountain frequently plunges sheer into the water, both pass swiftly from tunnel to corbelled structure and back again. Opposite Gravedona, between Colico and Corenno Plinio, a lofty elongated tongue of land encloses what is almost a small lake

THE CLOISTER IN THE ABBEY OF PIONA.

THE TOMBS OF THE CONTI ANDREANI, CORENNO PLINIO.

alongside the larger one. The eleventh-century Abbey of Piona stands on this eminence. It had been gradually abandoned before its suppression in 1798, and it was taken over again only at the beginning of the present century, this time by the Cistercians, who now make quite a reputable liqueur there. The church is in no way especially remarkable but the thirteenth-century cloister, with its white marble columns, surmounted by exquisitely carved capitals, is indeed of unusual elegance.

Another halt must be made at Corenno Plinio to see the three tombs of the Conti Andreani, backed by the church and the ancient castle : the quaintest Gothic fantasy in the whole region.

The best starting-point from which to climb Monte Legnone —

A REGATTA ON LAKE COMO.

A CARGO BOAT ON LAKE COMO.

THE SHORES OF LAKE COMO.

CHESTNUT TREES BESIDE LAKE COMO.

at 8528 feet the highest summit in the province — is Dervio on the broad delta of the Varrone torrent.

Bellano, too, is on a delta, at the mouth of the Valsassina. Its church of Santi Nazaro e Celso, with its alternate courses of black and white marble, reminds one of Florentine buildings. Slender cypresses rising behind it on the hillside emphasize the resemblance to a Tuscan landscape.

The prettiest portion of the eastern shore begins after Bellano. Opposite Menaggio and Bellagio it seems to have tried to achieve harmony. Varenna, amidst luxuriant gardens, is a very popular resort. The Fiumelatte is one of the shortest mountain torrents in Italy. For several months, in spring and above all in autumn, it tumbles down the mountain in a foaming cascade, which looks exactly like a river of milk.

Leaving Varenna, we enter the least interesting arm of the lake, that of Lecco, quite different in character from the other two. Dull and lifeless, shut in by steep mountains, its banks take on an air of indefinable hostility, especially when one has just left the flower-strewn beauty of the other shore. Even the rocky hill of Bellagio overlooking it is a cliff that plunges straight into the waves.

Lecco, an industrial and commercial town of 40,000 inhabitants, has been made famous by Manzoni in his *Promessi Sposi*. The only picturesque sight is a ten-arched stone bridge, built in 1336. But this has been ruined by recent widening. It crosses the Adda which forms a little lake, Lake Garlate, beyond Lecco. At the precise point where the Adda flows out of the lake the banks are connected by a great modern bridge opened in 1956.

●

A hilly, fertile region, the Brianza, stretches to the south of Monte San Primo between the Como and Lecco branches of the lake. It has always been delightful here though before the advent of the automobile made the district easily accessible it was almost completely unknown to foreigners.

The drive from Milan to Bellagio is most interesting. First one reaches Desio, birthplace of Pope Pius XI. I remember visiting the beautiful Villa Traversi here during the lifetime of Tomaso Tittoni who was for many years Italian Ambassador in Paris. The road then continues among lovely hills to Inverigo where one can see the Rotonda built, in 1833, by Cagnola, the architect who designed the Arco della Pace which adorns one entrance to Milan.

At the foot of the low hills which border the Plain of Lombardy we next come upon four small lakes that add greatly to the charm of this pleasing countryside where nature seems disposed to collaborate in providing for man's relaxation and delight instead of crushing him. The road passes between the lakes of Pusiano and Alserio and drops down to Erba whence it again climbs to Longone and Canzo, then to Asso where — geographically at least — the Brianza ends.

Then comes the Valassina and another climb as far as Magreglio and the Madonna del Ghisallo, standing among chestnut trees at a height

LECCO.

GARDENS OF BELLAGIO.

of 2473 feet. Then down again; and suddenly, with a twist in the road, one discovers the three branches of the lake. Seen from this height they look like sapphires set in circles of emeralds. The wonderful panorama, changing with every turn of the road, stretches right to the snow-capped Alpine summits. Bellagio extends at one's feet on its triangular shaped peninsula, like a snake's head resting on the water. The road drops in a series of vertiginous hairpin-bends among gardens which become increasingly luxuriant the closer one approaches to the lake. And so to Bellagio, one of the loveliest spots on earth and perhaps the most voluptuous in all Northern Italy.

Bellagio's situation is unique. The author of *La Chartreuse de Parme* praises it thus : " On the bold promontory that separates the two branches of the lake, that of Como so voluptuous, whereas the Lecco arm is harsh and austere : a sublime and gracious aspect equalled but by no means surpassed by the most famous spot in the world — the Bay of Naples. " It is a truly charming little town with its quayside arcades, its shops and public buildings, its streets rising in steps which lose themselves in greenery on the hillside, and its lithe peasant women. Some of these, though fewer every day, still clatter on the flagstones in their *zoccoli* — wooden sandals that cover only the tips of their toes. The thirteenth-century church of San Giacomo has three naves, a raised choir and three semicircular apses and is worth a visit. Beautiful villas with splendid gardens stretch between Bellagio and the little village of San Giovanni with its tall dignified cypresses, so often depicted by artists, marching down to the lake. The most famous villas are the Villa Melzi, filled with works of art, and enveloped in dark trees brightened by marble statuary; the Villa Poldi Pezzoli, with a mausoleum of the last Gonzago; the Villa Giulia, whose façade looks out over the Lecco branch of the lake, with beautiful flower-beds and stately groves.

But the glory of Bellagio is the former Villa Serbelloni; now a luxury hotel, whose gardens skirt the shores of the marvellous promontory and command views over the three arms of *Lacus Larius* in turn. To realize their attraction one must stroll at the end of a September afternoon along the paths bordered with trailing plants — camellias, magnolias, myrtles, pomegranates with trunks gnarled like plaited ropes, orange and lemon trees, steely blue cacti erect as swords, enormous fleshy-leaved aloes. The oleanders sag beneath the weight of their clusters. The overheated earth and the clumps of flowers give out clouds of odours and perfumes such as one inhales on any warm morning in the humid

AT BELLAGIO.

atmosphere of the Mercato Nuovo at Florence. And above all these exhalations the *olea fragrans* sheds its powerful aroma : no flowering tree emits a subtler, more pervasive odour than this far-eastern olive that has been acclimatized on these shores. At every step, through the

THE PARK OF THE VILLA TRIVULZIO, SAN GIOVANNI DI BELLAGIO.

thickets of leaves bordering the paths, views open out over Bellagio, a diamond which enhances the emerald richness of the three lakes that form its setting, and over the villages stretched out beside the water like idle women.

•

On the uppermost terrace, on the very summit of the promontory, a spot whence the eye takes in the lake's northern shores as if from the prow of a tall ship, the graceful silhouettes of umbrella pines break the skyline. They have an air of solemnity when lit from below by the oblique rays of the setting sun. A bluish haze begins to blur the forms of the surrounding gardens. The wrinkled surface of the lake under the hill reflects the purples and golds of the sunset-bathed country-side, shimmering like shot silk. The light-haloed villages lie at rest along the vermilion-flushed banks. Varenna, close to the outlet of the Val d'Esino, stretches itself among its cool gardens. One can still see in imagination the course of the Fiumelatte, although the heat of summer suns has stilled the torrent. Near the water, on the railway line hewn out of the naked rock beside the winding corniche road, glide the trains to Lecco or to Colico. From this distance they are just like a child's toys : they plunge into tunnels so short at times that the engines emerge before the last carriages have entered them. To the north, tenuous light-coloured patches clustered on the banks like flocks of gulls mark the whereabouts of far-off villages. Each white boat ploughs a sparkling furrow that widens to infinity.

My favourite nook is beneath the great oak which overshadows the terrace near the hotel. How many hours I once spent there fifty years ago, while writing *L'amour sous les lauriers-roses*. Between the marble balustrade, with its swollen blood-red veins, and the thin screen of motionless leaves, placed like the downstage wing of a theatre set, the Lecco and Como branches of the lake quiver in the light.

There are few panoramas in Italy more perfect in composition or harmony. Admittedly the view of Florence from either Fiesole or San Miniato, and the gentle Umbrian valley contemplated from the summit of Giardino di Frontone, at Perugia, move one more deeply. But most certainly no other view is so fascinating. One might even say reproachfully that it is too sensuous in appeal, too physical, in a way. Nowhere else can one more readily understand Flaubert's statement that " there

160

are some spots on earth which one longs to clasp to one's bosom ".

The shores of Lake Como are like beautiful girls gathered to welcome us, resembling those nymphs described by Politian in his *Stanze*, who step forward bearing armfuls of flowers and whose lithe and gentle bearing he praises in the almost untranslatable words, *il dolce andar soave...*

A COPY OF CANOVA'S CUPID AND PSYCHE GROUP IN THE VILLA CARLOTTA.

BESIDE LAKE ISEO.

MONTISOLA, LAKE ISEO.

Chapter Six

LAKE ISEO

Just as the little lakes of Orta and of Varese are neglected because
of Lake Maggiore, so Lake Iseo, which seems in a way to epitomize
all the others, is too often neglected for the more attractive Lake Garda.
It has patches of vegetation as luxuriant as its illustrious neighbour or
Lake Como, beauty-spots wilder than those of Lake Lugano and, like
Lake Maggiore, an imposing background of mountains with the snow-

THE ROAD BESIDE LAKE ISEO.

capped peaks of the Adamello massif, the Pian di Nive and the distant glaciers of Salarno. Tiny though it is, it yet indulges in the luxury of an island, the largest lake island in Italy, the Montisola.

I have always had a tender spot for this corner of Italy over which hovers a memory of France. On these banks " whose surroundings, " wrote George Sand, " are mild and refreshing as an Eclogue by Virgil ", she spent several weeks enveloped in tumultuous dreams and she put something of herself — perhaps a great deal — into her novel of the ill-fated love affair of Prince Carol of Roswald and the comedienne Lucrezia Floriani.

I feel that the novelist exaggerated the idyllic appearance of this lake, the towns of which have some quite busy industries.

The former *Lacus Sabinus* of the Romans is formed by the river Oglio descending from the Val Camonica. The dolomitic ridge of the Monte Guglielmo overlooks it on the west and separates it from the Val Trompia. Never greater than two and a half miles wide, it is over fifteen and a half miles long. There is much of interest along the roads that encircle it : we will follow them instead of using the boat which plies between its shores.

If one approaches the lake by the road from Brescia, one can pause briefly at Provaglio d'Iseo to have a glimpse of an eleventh-century monastery, with squat walls and stumpy campanile rising from a vast peat-bog. Some extremely interesting frescoes have recently come to light here during restoration.

Iseo, after which the lake is named, is of no greater importance than other villages on its banks, such as Pisogne or Lovere, which we shall shortly be visiting. It is a peaceful little town strung out along the shore, with a thirteenth-century church of which only the ancient façade and the campanile rising over the tombs of the Oldofredi family now remain. On the altar of one of the chapels within, one must examine a canvas representing *St Michael*, the masterpiece of the Venetian artist Francesco Hayez, one of the innovators of the Romantic Movement in Italy.

The northward road from Iseo skirts the lake's eastern shore, passing through Sulzano, a holiday resort favoured by Brescians, whence it is easy to reach the island of Montisola by boat, next Marasino, where there are large blanket-making factories, and then Marone, a fairly busy tourist centre, whose church boasts several works of art, notably a canvas of the *Redeemer* by Pietro da Marone.

The most interesting excursion one can make from these villages

PISOGNE.

is the climb up Monte Guglielmo (6396 feet) from the summit of which one sees a truly magnificent view.

Pisogne is quite an important summer holiday resort, but still more important as the centre of many industries. In its church, the former

Augustinian monastery of Santa Maria delle Neve, one can admire frescoes by Romanino, as well as a strange *Danse Macabre*.

Lovere, a very busy town, with equally important industries, deserves an hour or two of one's time. It is the prettiest town on the shores of this lake, in a wonderful position at the foot of some hills which protect it from cold winds. Its late fifteenth-century parish church of Santa Maria in Valvendra possesses some pictures by local artists; but one can afford to neglect these in order to devote rather more time to the palace of the Accademia Tadini where the collections of the Museo Tadini, the most important in the district, have been installed. Most

REEDS IN LAKE ISEO.

of the painters of Brescia, Verona and Venice are represented here, notably Bellini, Pâris Bordone, Palma the Younger, Tintoretto and Moretto. One can also see the plaster model of the statue of *Religion* which Canova made for the monument of Clement XIII in Rome, and some porcelain specimens from Capodimonte, from France, from Dresden and from the Far East. In the garden of the Palazzo Cappella there is another quite notable sculpture by Canova, a cenotaph commemorating a member of the Tadini family.

If one has a spare day, a trip to the high plateau of Bossico will provide views over the whole countryside.

Travelling southwards down the length of the western shore which belongs to Bergamo province, beyond Castro one comes upon a picturesque gorge with curious calcareous stratifications; and then Riva di Solto whose quarries of black marble supplied the columns of St Mark's in Venice. Riva di Solto is the starting-point for many climbs up the hills surrounding the town. And although those seldom exceed a height of 4 000 feet, they nevertheless command extensive and extremely varied landscapes.

Next comes the tiny city of Tavernola which I remember seeing, in the spring of 1906, overwhelmed by dismay and sorrow. A part of the town had slipped and disappeared under the water. As I had lunched there some months previously beneath a bower of roses, this picture of death in the midst of the splendours of nature moved me deeply. I pondered Lucretius' *Surgit amari aliquid* and also that fancy of Barrès', when he wished that the cemeteries of the Italian lakeside villages could be situated right beside the water so that they might be caressed by the waves thrown up on the banks by the cheerful boats. These gloomy visions would have added poignancy to lovers' delights. It is surely natural that sensual pleasure is enhanced by the thought that it is perishable — that it may be snatched away forever in a matter of seconds.

Tavernola, its disasters made good, is today a tourist centre equally suitable as a starting-point for ascents to some of the peaks just mentioned.

Having rounded the majestic Punta del Corno we pass through Predore, a place of some importance in Roman times as is shown by numerous ruins beneath present-day buildings; and finally we reach Sarnico at the southern tip of the lake near the out-flowing river Oglio, a tributary which enters the Po near the Mincio.

Beyond the Oglio, facing Predore, is Paratico where, according to legend, Dante once stayed in the Castel degli Lantieri.

To complete our tour of the lake we must take the steamer or hire boat in order to visit the island of Montisola which is, as I have already said, the largest island in the Italian Lakes. It is about six miles in circumference and the feature which gives it such a picturesque appearance is the sheer drop into the water, especially on the eastern side. The summit rises to about 1968 feet which is more than 1312 feet above the level of the lake. Two little harbours contain its few hundred inhabitants, almost all of whom are fisherfolk or net-makers : Siviano on the north and Peschiera Maraglio to the south. On the summit, the shrine of the Madonna della Seriola offers a very fine view across the lake and over the Alps of Bergamo. On certain days in late spring-time, when the atmosphere is crystal clear, these Alpine peaks stand out sharply against a blue sky so pale that it resembles a water-colour. The highest crests, still powdered with snow, seem to dissolve into the pale azure.

A CAMPANILE ON THE EASTERN SHORE OF LAKE ISEO.

TORBOLE.

NETS DRYING IN THE GOLFO DI SALO.

CHAPTER SEVEN

LAKE GARDA

When one has extolled the beautiful and picturesque features of Lake Maggiore and Lake Como, it seems that all one's faculties for admiration are exhausted and that a new lake can have nothing more for us to marvel at. But we have only to reach the edge of Lake Garda and observe its shores to realize at once that the former *Lacus Benacus*,

171

beloved of Virgil, Horace and Catullus, yields nothing to its neighbours and surpasses them in its incomparable majesty. It is the largest of the Italian lakes, being over thirty-one miles long and up to twelve miles wide. Its northern extremity, narrow and very deep, recalls the fiords of Norway. The southern end, on the other hand, resembles a small sea tossed by winds and sometimes thrown up into great waves. "Lake Garda," wrote Renan to his friend Berthelot, "is glorious : it is the

THE CYPRESSES OF THE PUNTA DI SAN VIGILIO.

GARDA. HARBOUR AND THE ROCCA DI GARDA.

most beautiful of the Alpine lakes of Italy. This trough surrounded by huge piled-up mountains is an altogether remarkable phenomenon. " Luxuriant vegetation clothes its shores. Lemon, orange and citron trees flourish in the open air in the warmest, most sheltered nooks. Real forests of olive trees cover the hillsides. Caper bushes grow from every wall crevice and the paths are shaded by enormous oleanders.

If one would rather avoid being restricted solely to the steamer

IN THE HARBOUR OF SAN VIGILIO.

when visiting the lake — and as it is so extensive this requires many days — I strongly advise those tourists with a car to start from Verona and make a roundabout journey in order to go up to the revered shrine of the Madonna della Corona, by way of Affi, with a passing salutation for the magnificently shaded Villa Poggi, and Caprino Veronese. From the narrow terrace before the church of the Corona, situated

PORTO DI BRENZONE.

THE CASTLE OF THE SCALIGERS AT MALCESINE (XIIITH TO XIVTH C.).

perpendicularly above the Adige valley, one can enjoy a very picturesque view of a loop of this river hemmed in by high cliffs.

A swift descent brings one down to the lakeside at Bardolino, noted for its vineyards, and at Garda, a former Roman town which prides itself on having given the lake its name. The Rocca here is the remnant

LOOKING INTO THE SETTING SUN, LAKE GARDA.

OLIVE TREES NEAR MALCESINE.

TORBOLE FROM THE LAKE.

TORBOLE.

YUCCAS GROWING BESIDE LAKE GARDA.

of the ancient fortress which overlooked the entire eastern shore and of the castle of Berengar of Ivrea who, after defeating the Carolingians, claimed the crown of Italy. It was here that he imprisoned Adelaide, widow of the Italian king Lothario, until she was set free by Otto the Great. In the church of Santa Maria one may see some paintings by Palma the Younger. One should also have a look at the Villa Canossa and the Villa Albertini where, in 1848, Carlo-Alberto received the results

THE TOWN AND SURROUNDINGS OF RIVA DI GAR

OM THE CABLE-CAR STATION ON THE BASTIONE.

RIVA. THE CASTLE.

of the plebiscite for the annexation of Lombardy and Piedmont. Garda, formerly so peaceful, has become a kind of holiday resort for the people of the region, especially for the motorists of Verona, Brescia and even

Milan who come there for week-ends, to take part in sailing events of all kinds. Many hotels and some delightful restaurants beside the harbour have made a very lively little town of what was once a haven of peace and quiet.

From Bardolino to San Vigilio the roads are lined with huge cypresses, among the most venerable I know. Those of the Punta di San Vigilio especially have been widely used on posters, post-cards and pictures. This famous headland deserves its renown. You should stop in the shade of the giant chestnut trees just opposite Sirmione and peer through their branches at the deep blue lake sparkling in the sunshine. It is as if thousands of silver-scaled fish were performing a silent ballet for you.

But the pearl of this Punta di San Vigilio is the simple yet perfect Villa Guariente designed by San Micheli at the beginning of the sixteenth century for the lawyer Brenzone. Here again the cypresses are magni-

UNDER THE ARCHES, AT RIVA.

THE QUAYSIDE AT RIVA.

THE CASTEL D'ARCO.

ficent, and from the spacious loggia which looks out over the lake there are two of the finest views imaginable, of the shore towards Garda in one direction and towards Gardone in the other.

After San Vigilio, instead of following the road which runs along

TUNNELS OF THE GARDESANA OCCIDENTALE. WITH RIVA IN THE BACKGROUND.

EMERGING FROM A TUNNEL ON THE GARDESANA.

the shore of the lake, which is comparatively uninteresting here, one
must climb up over the slope as far as San Zeno di Montagna, a delightful
summer resort nearly 2000 feet up, from which almost the whole lake is

A PERGOLA AT LIMONE.

visible, from the Plain of Desenzano and Peschiera right to the precipitous banks of Riva with the snow-covered Adamello mountain mass in the background.

•

At length we come to Malcesine, one of the most celebrated and picturesque places on this eastern bank. To reach it we cross the peaceful Val di Sogno where there are villas hidden among flowers and greenery that seem like so many retreats built especially for the bliss of lovers. A tiny island, hardly more than a screen of trees above the lake, bears the same poetic name.

THE BAY OF MADERNO.

Writers, artists and dreamers have for centuries adored Malcesine. The romantic appearance of this little town captivates you immediately, the moment you glimpse its bright houses crouching around the foot of its crenellated castle and the diminutive harbour full of fishing boats with great ochre-coloured sails. In the parish church there are some good canvases by painters of the schools of Verona and Brescia, notably an *Entombment* by Girolamo dai Libri. The old palazzo of the Captains of the Lake has a massive façade adorned with arcaded windows framed in elegant pillars. It is now the town hall and a vast fresco in the principal chamber depicts the armorial bearings of the Venetian magistrates who used to preside there.

One of these captains, in an excess of zeal, arrested Goethe as an Austrian spy at the end of the eighteenth century, as the author of *Faust* humorously recounts in his *Italian Tour*. He contrived to exculpate himself by claiming to be a citizen of the Republic of Frankfurt; but he makes this curious observation, which his compatriots might well have pondered : " Man is an odd creature : with the sole aim of trying to adapt the world to suit himself, he creates for himself troubles and dangers just where it would have been so easy to see and enjoy in comfort and security. " An inscription marks the spot where he was arrested by the authorities in September 1786 :

HINC

J. W. GOETHE

ARCEM DELINEAVIT

He was, in fact, sketching the picturesque castle, which had greatly attracted him. A marble plaque marks the house opposite the town hall where he stayed on September 13 and 14, 1786.

The castle of the Scaligers, the silhouette of which so happily dominates the lake and the town, is worth visiting, if only for the superb view of the whole northern end of the lake from the little balcony that overhangs it. Like a black triangle between Torbole and Riva looms the dark crag of Monte Brione.

Malcesine is most frequently the point of departure for the climb up Monte Baldo, the renowned mountain whose gigantic undulating ridge sprawls all along the eastern shore of the lake. It takes four or five hours to reach the highest point, at 7478 feet.

A great calcareous fault-scarp runs obliquely down the mountainside into the lake : the shore is precipitous, wild and thoroughly inhospitable,

FASANO.

THE VITTORIALE OF GABRIELE D'ANNUNZIO.

and there are no villages along the road. So one hails with joyful exuberance the sight of Torbole, so luminous, so southern is the appearance of its brightly coloured houses. One can appreciate the enthusiasm with which many Nordic tourists greet these enchanted shores when they come upon them suddenly from the Tyrol. Even when Torbole was still Austrian (the former frontier used to lie between Malcesine and Torbole) they had the impression that they were already in Italy, the very name of which sent Heinrich Heine into ecstasies.

It was at Torbole — which one should not leave without visiting

A STORM ON LAKE GARDA; IN THE DISTANCE, GARDONE AND MADERNO.

GARDONE RIVIERA.

its beautiful, romantic cemetery — that Goethe set out for Malcesine,
where his journey to Italy began so inauspiciously. " This morning, "
he wrote, " I left for Italy in a boat with one pair of oars; the weather
was fine, though the sky was overcast; we were able to spread our sail

before a favourable wind. " It seems, doesn't it, as if we are listening to Ulysses describing one of his journeys on the cerulean sea ? " Happy waves that bear this little boat, " cried Maurice Barrès, " early sunbeams that touch the swaying treetops : favoured long ago by Virgil — now that the German poet has perceived you, henceforth you will sparkle down the ages as you dance on Tauris' imaginary strand... " Is it not thrilling to think that it was here in this little harbour of Torbole that

THE CYPRESSES OF THE ISOLA SAN BIAGIO.

Goethe had his first experience of Italy, here that his eyes were first opened to beauty, as were those of his Faust to his regained youth ? Here, too, Goethe had the first idea for his new Iphigenia who should awaken from herself in the thickets of magnolias that bend over *Lacus Benacus*.

Riva stands at the extreme tip of the lake beneath the gloomy Rocchetta which contrasts so strangely with the bright houses of the town and the gaiety of the harbour. In the ancient city, where some

FISHERMEN AT PORTESE.

THE ISOLA DI GARDA.

THE HARBOUR, DESENZANO.

foundations date back to Roman times, one notes especially the piazza surrounded by buildings recalling the sovereignty of Venice and the glorious house of the Scaliger family. The lakeside gardens are lavishly maintained : I always admire one beautiful magnolia avenue there.

Riva, which is admirably situated at the terminus of the roads which lead down from the Trentino and the Dolomites, becomes more important as a tourist centre every year. It is the most obvious starting and finishing point for journeys on the lake or in the surrounding mountains. One of the most popular excursions nowadays is the five-minute trip by cable-car *(seggiovia)* to the Bastione whence visitors can enjoy a beautiful and very extensive view over Riva and Torbole at the edge of the lake, over Arco and its castle not far away, and beyond to the chain of mountains rising in the background.

Beyond Riva the western coast as far down as Gargnano is even more rugged and inhospitable than the eastern shore between Malcesine and Torbole. Impressive walls of rock plunge steeply into the lake : they look superb, especially in the morning when lit by the fiery rays of the rising sun. Prior to the construction of the new road skirting the lake there were only a few wretched almost inaccessible hamlets on the mountainside. One little green patch, with a few houses, at the water's edge used to be called " Hungry Meadow " because it could be supplied with provisions only by boat — and even this could not be done at all when the storms, so common on Lake Garda at certain seasons, were at their fiercest.

Today the " Gardesana Occidentale ", begun in 1931, runs alongside the lake from Riva to Salô; with its eighty tunnels driven through the rock it is one of the finest roads in Italy, matching the " Gardesana Orientale ", the link between Peschiera and Riva, which we have already traversed. As it leaves Riva it passes below another magnificent, much older road, the " Ponale Road ", hewn out of the mighty rock walls of the Rocchetta, between the years 1848 and 1851 ; but it swerved away from the lake, after the mouth of the torrent which gave it its name.

Limone is a fishing hamlet in the centre of a tiny bay protected by huge cliffs. This village takes its name from many lemon plantations situated on the tiered terraces. The church contains some interesting canvases.

I strongly advise motorists who have plenty of confidence in themselves and their machines to tackle, before they reach Campione, the narrow road that enters the Tremosine by way of the deep gorges of the Val Brasa. I know of no more daring road. In places it is quite as impressive as that of Combe-Laval in the Dauphiné forest of Lente.

And what a marvellous viewpoint is this terrace of Pieve di Tremosine situated over 1 000 feet up, perpendicularly above the lake ! It is the finest — at all events the most awe-inspiring — in the region. On the other shore, exactly opposite, one sees the harbour of Malcesine and the eight summits of Monte Baldo.

Almost equally intense emotions will be experienced if, a little

AT PESCHIERA.

further on along the coast, one takes the track leading to Tignale, a charming summer resort. From here one can reach the Madonna di Monte Castello by following a road marked with numerous votive shrines.

At Gargnano the natural scenery suddenly changes. Gardens, villas with coloured façades, plantations of olive trees, lemon trees and citron trees give this shore a completely southern appearance. The Franciscan monastery with its Gothic cloister and the church of San Francesco are both worth visiting.

Now comes an almost unbroken succession of built-up areas beside the lake; first Bogliaco, with the palace of the Conti Bettoni; then Toscolano, with important paper mills; and lastly Maderno, a very popular holiday resort full of hotels and villas. This little town formerly belonged to Venice, as is shown by a column surmounted by the lion of St Mark on the quayside. Behind this rises the pleasing façade of the church of Sant'Andrea, built in the twelfth century on the ruins of a temple to Apollo. To the left, on an extremely tall pedestal, stands the statue of Sant'Ercolano, local patron saint and one-time protector of the whole lake.

After the impressive Zanardelli Garden and a series of fine villas

A SMALL BOAT ON LAKE GARDA.

we reach Fasano and Gardone Riviera, two jewels of Lake Garda which must be visited. Between these two stands the Vittoriale where Gabriele d'Annunzio spent his last years and died in 1938. I am deeply moved

THE RAMPARTS OF PESCHIERA.

THE CASTEL DI LAZISE.

when I muse upon my visits to the Vittoriale, especially the first : this occurred before he had undertaken the labours which were to transform into a kind of solemn pantheon the modest dwelling to which he retired after the Fiume expedition. After his death the architect Maroni carried on the work: the Vittoriale has become a kind of great museum where it is most difficult to rediscover the setting in which the author of *Il Fuoco* lived.

After Gardone the shore hollows out into a gulf at the head of which is Salò, a town retaining some traces of its past : in the days of Venetian supremacy it had its share of glory. In September 1943 it was the seat of the short-lived Fascist government of the " Republic of Salò ". The fifteenth-century cathedral of Santa Maria Annunziata is one of the most interesting religious buildings erected beside the lake : among the works of art that adorn it there are some canvases by Palma the Younger, Moretto and above all by Romanino,

LAKE GARDA AT SIRMIONE.

notably a beautiful *Madonna with the Saints Sebastian and Bonaventura.*

In the open lake of the Gulf of Salò a narrow, sombre tongue of land, the Isola di Garda, emerges from the water. It is a park whose magnificent trees shelter the Palazzo Dei Ferrari, owned nowadays by the Borghese family. The vast chambers of the Venetian-style mansion house a collection of pictures and antiquities, but it is hardly ever possible to see them or to enter the gardens.

●

Beyond the island, the coast reveals a marked contrast with the rugged shores we have just traversed. It is no more than an undulating plain covered with gardens, vines and orchards of great fertility. The vineyards yield a famous red wine, which goes by the name of " Riviera ". Only the black Rocca di Manerba jutting out into the lake breaks the monotony of the landscape.

The wide southern gulf, whose opposite shores are almost twelve and a half miles apart, is more like a sea — as Virgil's lines describe it :

fluctibus et fremitu adsurgens. Benace, marino.

On the landward side — as flat as the lake — one sees nothing on the horizon save the towers set up on the battlefields of San Martino and Solferino : sonorous names that call to mind the struggles endured by France's soldiers for Italian independence.

There is nothing more of special note as far as Desenzano. This is a very important tourist centre since it is the station on the Milan-Venice railway that serves Lake Garda and because its harbour is the departure and arrival point for the steamer services. If one has an hour to spare one might visit the church of Santa Maria Maddalena which contains some good canvases, in particular an excellent *Last Supper* by Tiepolo.

If we follow the straight motor road we very swiftly reach Peschiera, which is both a station on the Milan-Venice railway and the terminus of a branch line from Mantua. The river Mincio flows out of Lake Garda at Peschiera, a town whose position has at all times been of great strategic importance. The exceptional position of this beautiful and powerful citadel at the spot where the shore is at its lowest level, and covering the territories of Brescia and Bergamo, was celebrated long ago by Dante :

*Siede Peschiera,
bello e forte arnese*

*Da fronteggiar
Bresciani e Berga-
maschi,*

*Onde la riva intorno
piu discese.*

In all Italy's wars, the fortress of Peschiera has played its part as one of the four strongholds guarding the routes into Lombardy. Its enormous red brick walls surrounded by water make a compellingly romantic appeal to the eye. In the past I have many times longed to stop there because I had glimpsed it from the carriage window when travelling to Venice. And the visits I have subsequently had occasion to make have proved that I was right.

So, travelling northwards up the

THE GREAT WALLS
OF THE SCALIGERS'
CASTLE.

eastern shore from Peschiera we shall complete the circuit at Bardolino where we originally approached the Lake from Verona. There is little else of interest to note except the pretty little nook of Lazise, where the ruined walls of the Scaliger family's ancient castle call to mind the illustrious family whose history is linked with that of the lake.

●

We have one more excursion yet to make : I have kept it till last because it has about it a charm that *literati* will appreciate : a trip to the long promontory of Sirmione far out in the lake between Desenzano and Peschiera.

To appreciate this pleasure to the full one must approach Sirmione not by steamer but by the land route which runs the entire length of the narrow tongue of land to the little town at its extremity. Its houses are clustered around the crenellated castle whence the Scaliger family used to keep watch over the lake. Unused since then, it is a perfect comic opera set. Crowded with tourists and full of modern hotels, Sirmione nevertheless remains extremely picturesque with its alleys of angular paving stones bridged by archways, its flowering terraces, its little gardens of oleanders contrasting with the blue skies and waters.

In one's haste to reach what is called the Grotta di Catullo — so great is the prestige conferred by a poet upon the places he has extolled — one has little time for the town. Can those ruined walls at the extreme tip of the promontory really be the remains of the foundations of his villa ? Quite possibly so, for the writer would naturally have chosen the best possible position for his country residence.

Salve, o venusta Sirmio !

There was no better site, none more certain to attract the Latin poet : for again one remembers the delightful lines of Carducci on the subject :

Ecco : la verde Sirmio nel lucido lago sorride,
fiore delle penisole.

It is indeed the flower of the peninsula, and the Italian Government has very wisely designated it a protected area, in order to prevent its spoliation by the building of smart hotels. This pleasant yet imposing spot to which I have come to spend the last of the days I am devoting

THE SCALIGERS' CASTLE AT SIRMIONE.

THE RUINED REMAINS OF THE ROMAN VILLA OF CATULLUS, SIRMIONE.

to the Italian Lakes simply must be preserved for olives and fig trees,
ivies and sweet scented mints. Its position is reminiscent of the Bellagio
promontory; indeed it dominates the whole lake : the two curving bays
of the Veronese and Brescian shores and the long gulf stretching away
between the mountains as far as Riva. The eastern coast slopes gently

CLIFFS AT SIRMIONE.

above Lazise and the beautiful Punta di San Vigilio to the mighty naked ridge of Monte Baldo beyond. To the left the flower-decked banks of Salò, Gardone and Maderno sprawl in the shelter of Monte Pizzocolo : seen from here the crest of this mountain no longer quite suggests the profile of a recumbent Napoleon as it does from the road just outside Verona. To left and right the picture is framed, so to speak, by the two rock formations of Garda and Manerba. At the very foot of the point on which I am standing the flat rocks at water level appear like the low-relief plan of some ancient submerged town. The foam-flecked water is transparently green, deepening to an intense blue in the middle of the lake.

What a vision of beauty — at once exciting and restful. In the midst of all the restless anxieties of humanity and the upheavals that shake our civilization, how delightful to live, for one moment, in the everlasting tranquillity of nature. From the summit of this very promontory Catullus looked upon this same countryside, in whose life two thousand years are but as one day in ours.

THE COAT-OF-ARMS OF GEORGE, BISHOP OF NEUDEK, AT RIVA.

INDEX

Names of persons are printed in italics.

Figures in bold type refer to pages of illustrations.

THE CASA DEI CAPITANI DI LAGO, GARDA.

A CORNER OF THE HARBOUR, GARDA.

ACKNOWLEDGMENTS

PHOTOGRAPHS FOR THIS BOOK WERE TAKEN BY

S. ALINARI, Florence
Pages 42, 43, 104, 105, 108, 109, 117.

M. B. ARTHAUD, Paris
Pages, 16, 17, 19, 20, 21, 26, 35, 36, 47, 49, 55, 91, 136, 161, 172, 173, 174, 179, 181, 182-183, 187, 189, 202, 220, 221.

Mme Jacques ARTHAUD, Paris
Pages 8, 15.

M. M. AUDRAIN, Nantes
Pages, 9, 10, 14, 23, 24-5, 30, 32, 33, 34, 37, 39, 40, 45, 57, 66, 69, 75, 77, 80, 81, 85, 113, 114, 115, 116, 128, 130-1, 132, 133, 139, 140-1.

M. BOMBART, Saint-Quentin
Page 76.

M. BOUDOT-LAMOTTE, Paris
Pages 94, 196, 197.

S. BRUNNER, Como.
Page 193.

ENTE PROVINCIALE PER IL TURISMO, Varese
Page 51.

FOTOCELERE, Turin
Page 68.

S. Giulio GALIMBERTI, Milan
Pages 118, 119, 120, 121, 122, 123, 146, 150, 151, 153, 171, 195, 198.

M. GELLOS, Grenoble
Page 78.

Mlle JOURDE, Grenoble
Page 211.

M. MARMOUNIER, Aix-les-Bains
Pages 65, 95.

S. Riccardo MONCALVO, Turin
Pages 46, 56, 59, 60, 62, 64, 67, 71, 72, 73, 74, 82, 83, 84, 87, 88, 90, 93, 111.

S. Fernando PASTA, Milan
Pages 50, 52, 54, 97, 112, 124, 125, 126, 129, 134, 135, 142, 145, 148, 149, 158, 159, 180, 190, 194, 199, 200, 205, 213.

S. H. RUEDI, Lugano
Pages 58, 98-9, 100, 102.

S. Ch. SHIEFER, Lugano
Pages 106-7.

S. Bruno STEFANI, Milan
Pages 28, 127, 152, 155, 156, 162, 163, 164, 166, 167, 169, 170, 175, 208-9.

S. E. STEINEMANN, Locarno
Page 61.

M. Antoine TRINCANO, Lyons
Pages 11, 12-13, 29, 176, 177, 178, 184, 185, 186, 188, 191, 203, 204, 206, 212, 214.